ROOMS TO INSPIRE IN THE CITY

ROOMS TO INSPIRE IN THE CITY

STYLISH INTERIORS FOR URBAN LIVING

ANNIE KELLY

PHOTOGRAPHY BY TIM STREET-PORTER

RIZZOLI
NEW YORK

Anybody can be good in the country.
There are no temptations there.

—Oscar Wilde
The Picture of Dorian Gray

ACKNOWLEDGMENTS

Rooms to Inspire in the City would not have been possible without the help of our many friends—Robert Couturier, Peter Dunham, Muriel Brandolini, Jaya Ibrahim, John and Cynthia Hardy, David Cruz, Liv Ballard, Zang Toi, and Florence de Dampierre. They were incredibly generous with their time and enthusiasm.

We are grateful to all the people who opened their houses and apartments to us, and would also like to thank Linda O'Keeffe at *Metropolitan Home* magazine and Nancy Butkus at the *New York Observer Home* magazine, where some of these places first appeared. Thanks also go to: Andrew Logan and Michael Davis, who invited Tim to stay in London; Simon Upton, who contributed an important photograph; Hutton Wilkinson, who helped with Dodie Rosekrans in Paris and all things Duquette; Martyn Lawrence-Bullard, who kindly flew Tim to London to photograph the apartment he designed for Tamara Mellon; and Made Wijaya, who lent us his house in Bali while we finished this book. We are also indebted to Mike Kelly, who helped with technical issues, and to Christin Markmann, who kept Tim's office running smoothly while we were traveling. Our Rizzoli team was Sandy Gilbert, David Huang, and Doug Turshen. As always, we aspire to their sensibility and professionalism.

PREVIOUS SPREAD: The ornate exterior of the nineteenth-century Ansonia building on New York's Upper West Side. RIGHT: The London drawing room of antiquarian Peter Hinwood.

CONTENTS

LEFT: *Peter Dunham and Peter Kopelson's dogs wait for a walk at the back door of their West Hollywood bungalow.*

THE INFINITE POSSIBILITIES FOR DESIGNING CITY ROOMS

WHAT INSPIRED THE DESIGN of these city apartments and small houses? It was perhaps the pleasurable challenge of making them visually as well as physically comfortable in order to provide a retreat—a place to step back from the outside world. After all, this is important in many urban areas, which are out of control, bustling with relentless traffic and unchecked development. Often the only part of the city that can be tamed is behind the front door. Here, we show a selection of ideas from the most creative people in the decorating world, who have designed their own city homes, as well as homes of their friends and clients.

In each of the previous *Rooms to Inspire* books we began with the work of one of today's most influential decorators, the late Tony Duquette. We couldn't resist showing how he stopped at nothing to bring an exotic richness to Dodie Rosekrans's Parisian pied-à-terre. Duquette shopped in India to create a pure fantasy, down to dramatic leopard-skin awnings decorating the exterior of the building.

The celebrated turn-of-the-last-century Dakota apartment building on Central Park West is among the finest living spaces that New York had to offer at the time. Finished in 1884, it has breathtakingly grand proportions, an open interior courtyard on the scale of the plaza of a small European town, and came with all sorts of modern conveniences, even a gym. Today, it is still one of the city's most desirable buildings, and we show a small ground-floor apartment with grand style and proportions,

recently decorated by Muriel Brandolini, who can make even a modest-size space look luxurious. Perhaps inspired by David Hicks's famous set in London's Albany, Brandolini also added moments of drama, like a draped four-poster bed right in the middle of where most people would expect a living room.

Another stately nineteenth-century New York building is the Ansonia. Inspired by French Beaux Arts architecture of the time, it was built as a residential hotel that included its own air-conditioning. Designer John Hardy and his wife Cynthia fell in love with its turrets and lavish interior architectural detailing. They bought a corner apartment to serve as a pied-à-terre on visits from their home in Bali. My favorite space is their Javanese bathroom, built with slatted wood that is lit from behind to look like sunlight streaming through the boards, with a shower that descends through the slats like a burst of rain. Zang Toi's Upper East Side apartment was also French-inspired, but was built as part of a grand town house with fine nineteenth-century proportions. During the same period, decorator Robert Couturier's building was constructed as office space downtown in SoHo. Not much has changed in a hundred years as he runs his business here, using a small apartment, tucked into one of its floors, as a garçonnière.

Some cities are more suburban in character, and these homes offer more space, as well as greater out-

Like the Chateau Marmont and the Chinese Theatre in Los Angeles, our house in the Hollywood Hills is an example of 1920s Hollywood fantasy architecture.

Villa
Vallombrosa
2074

door areas. Los Angeles is a classic twentieth-century city of this type, where many people's houses have gardens large enough to re-create the atmosphere of a small resort. Here, decorator Peter Dunham and his partner Peter Kopelson make use of both the indoors and outdoors around a small swimming pool. Mary McDonald converted her previous home in the Hollywood Hills into a guesthouse when she moved to Brentwood. In a Hollywood Regency Revival style, it was too beautiful to part with when she moved. Suburbia is worldwide: Designer Jaya Ibrahim lives in a single-floor Jakarta house, where he also maintains an office. The central courtyard includes a spa-like open bathroom—an enviable luxury in the tropics.

Most of the designers in this book have a considered relationship with the architecture of their homes. Even Duquette created a logical "backstory" for his place in San Francisco's Cow Hollow, imagining it to be the house of a ship's captain who had traveled the Orient, bringing back spoils from China and Thailand to furnish his home. Successful decorating generally follows the original architectural intent of the property, even if there is a certain amount of poetic license involved. However, some apartments can be like blank canvases for a personal story. For example, Muriel Brandolini gave Eric Hadar's modern penthouse in New York an Asian flavor. After high school, Hadar had spent a year traveling through the Orient, and today he is always happy to come home from work to a place that reminds him of his footloose and fancy-free youth.

THE ART OF INDIVIDUAL STYLE

Just as clothing reflects our personality and taste, our homes tell other people who we are. Even if we have brought in someone else to help us, how we decorate our home establishes a personal context combining where we live with our cultural enthusiasms and interests. Even changing one room in an apartment can be exciting, like turning over a new leaf. It gives a feeling of rebirth and a sense of countless new possibilities. To some extent, we all wear our houses like a turtle wears its shell, and a successful interior can be a reflection of ourselves—redo a room to become a different person. Designer Jonathan Adler recommends redecorating as his "prescription for anti-depressive living," as you can see here in the cheery Manhattan apartment he did for the Wagman family.

How can we create our own personal style? The good news is that there has never been so much raw material available, thanks to globalization and China's industrious factories. The design industry now caters to everyone, with both high and low versions of almost everything, from fabrics to furnishings of every sort. With the influx of affordable style in stores such as Pottery Barn, Ikea, and Target, good design is available for everyone.

Although their number is shrinking as a result of today's risky dependence on advertising, magazines show what is out there and how to put interiors together. Bloggers such as peakofchic.com, stylecourt.com, and rivieraview.com are stepping in to fill the creative void left by the demise of much loved publications like *Domino* and *House & Garden*. Magazines have also been hurt by the Internet, although many of the design blogs promote them by mentioning their favorite decorating stories every month. Some of the best blogs are as informative as picking up your favorite design magazine. What makes a good decorating blog? Daily postings cover a wide variety of finds and inspirations, written about with enthusiasm and passion that both entertain and educate. Unlike many of today's remaining shelter magazines, they aren't afraid to have a point of view.

Planned as an Italian-style piano nobile, our main living room is on the first floor. French and Italian eighteenth- and nineteenth-century furniture continues the illusion of a house in Europe.

Furniture from past eras is there for anyone who is prepared to search. The website 1stdibs.com offers page after page of great twentieth-century furniture, both mass-produced pieces like the designs of Charles Eames, or more rarified items like those of Jean-Michel Frank. Stores across America specialize in furniture from every period, and in most cities you can find a design district to provide hours of happy browsing.

Today's most obvious trend is to combine styles and periods to arrive at a personal synthesis of inspirations. Much like the decorating of the 1960s and seventies, many people are pairing modern furniture with period styles. However, we shouldn't forget that "modern" has been fashionable for almost ninety years, so by now there is a lot of room for experimentation. The current international trend seems to be large open spaces, sparsely furnished with perfectly tailored sofas, luxurious rugs, and a collection of contemporary art that varies from country to country. Today there is a Jeff Koons in every elegant living room—who knows who tomorrow's artist will be?

However, some people prefer a more cozy version of historicism. Ralph Lauren has mastered the style of the comfortable rich, with the illusion of an ancestral past. No one else has influenced how we dress and live as much as this quintessential designer who has identified various lifestyles, packed them up, and sold these utopian visions back to us. Decorators like Bunny Williams have been enormously influential across America, thanks to her best-selling books. Even if you find this decorating style conservative, her advice holds true no matter what style of apartment you have. Good decorating is an art, and the same principles apply before you begin to decide on color and style.

The work of early- and mid-century modern furniture designers has never been more popular, and many of them have been well documented in several recent books. Look out for *Paul Frankl*, by Christopher Long; *Class Act: William Haines*, by Peter Schifando and Jean Mathison; *Gio Ponti*, edited by Ugo La Pietra; and *Jean-Michel Frank*, by Pierre-Emmanuel Martin-Vivier. You can also find inspiration in other decorators' books that show their own urban interiors put together with great verve and skill. Apart from those that we show here, another big influence today is the spare and refined work of Belgian designer and collector Axel Vervoordt. He is a connoisseur of old and beautiful objects, which he mixes with the modern lines of contemporary art and design. Vervoordt has the eye of an artist and is an inspiration to many as an interior designer, collector, and dealer on a grand scale.

Abrasive as it is, why are we so attracted to big city living? People have always been drawn by the city's irresistible siren call of culture, trade, and society, including many of America's most successful designers, who make all sorts of compromises and often sacrifice space to live this way. Sadly, in New York, where maintaining whole town houses was once the norm, many today are usually carved up into small apartments. But there are always ways to add the illusion of extra space into these homes as we can see in today's town house balconies, the backyards of ivy-covered brownstones, and views of urban parks. In the more suburban cities, especially in warmer climates, the transition between indoors and outdoors is very important, and a well-furnished garden can expand the living space of the house.

Each of the rooms in this book has an element of design and decoration that we find inspiring. We hope you enjoy these ideas as much as we do. Above all, one of the greatest luxuries in the world is the peace and calm in one's own home.

A pair of Garouste and Bonetti bronze sconces flank an ancestral painting from Martyn Lawrence-Bullard in the living room. The draped table is an excellent place for authors like us to store magazine reference material underneath. FOLLOWING SPREAD: The city of Los Angeles spreads out from a view high in the Hollywood Hills.

PART I

City Rooms

THE LITTLE HOUSE OF FLOWERS

Tony Duquette's San Francisco Town House

TONY DUQUETTE WAS AN enormously prolific decorator, especially when it came to his own houses, which he worked on continuously and were never considered finished. Although he usually got his own way with clients, he could fume for years over small changes they summoned up the courage to ask him to make. In his own places, however, he was limited by nothing more than his own imagination—which, by anyone's standards, was endlessly fertile.

When Duquette was based in Los Angeles in the early 1950s, he had a groundbreaking Paris exhibition of his work travel to San Francisco's de Young Museum, and he found himself working in San Francisco, designing costumes for the city's ballet and opera companies. He realized with pleasure that he needed a base in the city—never forgetting for a moment that this would be another decorating opportunity. Acquired in the 1960s, with the residuals from *Camelot*, this turn-of-the-century Victorian town house in a district known as Cow Hollow, which slopes down to the bay, became his new project. Here was a chance for Duquette to make use of all the architectural salvage he had been storing, as this gingerbread-style house could take many extra layers of detail. He initially called it "The Little House of Flowers," although with each burst of decorating the style of the house took on a different direction.

Since San Francisco is famous for its harbor, Duquette based his design on the theme of a ship's captain returning to port with spoils from the mysterious East. He could even observe the sea from a "captain's cabin" and terrace garden that he had built on the roof. In the entryway, he created one of his most extraordinary displays: a kind of glassed-in set, like a diorama, featuring a spectacular Thai spirit house surrounded by salvaged Chinese carvings and moldings. Lit from above, this became a magical moment when guests first entered the house.

The dining room was anchored by a pair of eighteenth-century Austrian corner cabinets, fitted with portraits of Emperor Franz Joseph and his finance minister. Duquette covered a breakfront cabinet of his own design in Fortuny fabric topped with a carved Venetian lambrequin. Leading from this space were two dramatically marbleized living rooms—painted by his wife, Beegle (an accomplished artist herself), who worked on the entire ground-floor walls and ceilings. The walls are layered with hanging fabric panels, mirrors, and architectural fragments. Duquette believed in creating an atmosphere of richness with different kinds of detail, rather like a stage set, treating life as a performance. He also loved exotic furniture, and a set of nineteenth-century Egyptian Revival seating in the front room, found on a shopping trip with director Vincente Minnelli, provided a visual link with the period of the house.

Upstairs there were at least four bedrooms, which came in handy for visiting workers who helped on his projects. Here Duquette turned to his great love of the exotic and furnished the rooms with Chinese beds, furniture, and textiles. The master bedroom featured hand-painted Chinese wallpaper and a chandelier once made for Duquette's great patron, Elsie de Wolfe.

When Duquette redecorated the house in 1993, he stored some of the furnishings at his Malibu ranch, which subsequently burned down. As he sold this house before he died in 1999, the photographs that you see here are the only record of this extraordinary labor of love.

The Victorian exterior of Tony Duquette's San Francisco town house was extensively reworked by the designer.

ABOVE: *To the left of the entry, Duquette created this elaborate glassed-in tableau centered on several Thai spirit houses.* RIGHT: *The living room featured nineteenth-century Egyptian Revival seating, discovered on a shopping trip with director Vincente Minnelli. Beegle Duquette worked with friends to marbleize the entire room, including the fireplace.*

The dining room was anchored by a pair of eighteenth-century Austrian corner cabinets, fitted with portraits of Emperor Franz Joseph and his finance minister. Here, Duquette covered a breakfront cabinet of his own design in Fortuny fabric topped with a carved Venetian lambrequin.

ABOVE AND LEFT: Upstairs, a warren of rooms included another living room, this time decorated in the Asian style Duquette loved. You can see how he added fabrics and even used carved panels to decorate walls, creating a rich layered look.

A PARISIAN JEWEL

Dodie Rosekrans's Paris Apartment, Designed by Tony Duquette

WHEN SAN FRANCISCAN COLLECTOR and philanthropist Dodie Rosekrans bought her Paris pied-à-terre, she wanted to make a splash. But how would she get the French to notice yet another American in Paris? Her secret weapon was her old friend, the late decorator Tony Duquette. Rosekrans had met Duquette years before he was as well known as the style icon he is today. After she bought the Paris apartment, in the mid-1990s, she was inspired by a trip to Dawnridge, Duquette's extraordinary Beverly Hills house. There she encountered the fantasy she was looking for—perhaps too intense for everyday living (after all, her main house in San Francisco had been decorated by the great, and comparatively conservative, Michael Taylor) but perfect for a place where she spends several months a year.

It is hard to believe that this apartment is only 1,600 square feet, as the richness of detail is so intense. Much of Duquette's inspiration came from travels to India. A compulsive shopper, he had started making trips there after Rosekrans had brought him in to decorate a legendary party that she and her late husband held at the California Palace of the Legion of Honor in San Francisco. In a building donated by her husband's family, Duquette and his design partner, Hutton Wilkinson, created a tentlike Indian fantasy, rendering the original building unrecognizable. They proceeded to do the same with Rosekrans's Paris apartment, but added to the mix furnishings that both Duquette and his client had stored away. This pied-à-terre encompasses only four rooms, including a kitchen. When the apartment was documented by a photographer, Duquette exclaimed, "Don't photograph that room. Dodie's never been in it!"

One of Duquette's first principles was never to provide a place for the eye to rest. He layered everything he had on hand to create a feeling of being overpowered—the key, in his mind, to successful decorating. Rosekrans was a willing accomplice—she let him do what he wanted. This is vital for a creative spirit. When Duquette was free to dream, he was at his most original.

How they managed to add leopard-skin fabric awnings to the exterior of the 7th arrondissement building in the heart of conservative Paris was a mystery, and a source of constant amazement to most passersby. If you were lucky enough to gain admittance, you would be equally dazzled by the gold-leaf rotunda entrance. This leads to a deeply exotic dining room lined with a green damask print and hung with a dizzying array of mirrors, cleverly expanding the space through reflections of the adjoining rooms. The living room is lined with jeweled antique Indian textiles, and in a corner hangs a carved Thai mirror decorated with eyes—"the only mirror that looks back at you," said Duquette when it was installed. In the darkly rich master bedroom, an elaborate four-poster bed takes up most of the space. It is hung with an eclectic combination of silk brocade, Indian textiles, and a "discovered" canopy trimmed with the best French passementerie. To add reflection to the bedroom walls, Duquette seized with delight Rosekrans's eighteenth-century Venetian mirrored and gilt-wood panels for the walls, which she had bought from the late Rose Cummings.

When the design team returned to Duquette's Beverly Hills base, they worked with careful measurements of the apartment. It is important to get things right, as Wilkinson's motto was "measure twice and ship once." Happily everything fit once it arrived in Paris, and Rosekrans was ready to create a sensation.

Tony Duquette designed the unique living room mirror in Dodie Rosekrans's Paris apartment, incorporating antique Asian elements. He called it "the only mirror that looks back at you."

ABOVE: The window awnings were upholstered in a leopard-skin fabric for an extra touch of glamour. RIGHT: *The apartment is quite small, but Duquette's choice of fabrics and furnishings create a sumptuous effect. He upholstered the walls in the living room with a collection of antique mogul embroideries.*

*ABOVE: A silvered dressing table from India in the master bedroom.
RIGHT: Duquette and design partner Hutton Wilkinson chose to drape the bed
with a collection of antique red and green brocades, topped with a pelmet they
found at a Paris flea market. The mirror wall panels were bought by Rosekrans
from the estate of the late decorator Rose Cumming and shipped over to Paris.*

ABOVE: *The doors to the master bedroom were mirrored, helping to increase the illusion of a larger space. The torso is by Polish artist Bronislaw Krzysztof.*
RIGHT: *The bathroom was entirely paneled in pierced wooden screens backed with mirror, and Duquette covered the floor in a leopard-skin-patterned carpet.*

ABOVE: *A detail of the Rose Cumming mirrored wall panels in the master bedroom.*
RIGHT: *In the dining room, Duquette had the chairs custom-made in Rajastan. The extraordinary alligator chair is by French artist Claude Lalanne.*

BUNGALOW STYLE

Jaya Ibrahim's City Home in Jakarta, Indonesia

JAKARTA MAY SEEM A LONG WAY from almost everywhere, where the sound of the *adman*, or "call to prayer," echoes poetically over the smoggy skies, but here you will find the home of well-known international decorator Jaya Ibrahim. This is a huge, sprawling city—the political and financial center of the country—and Ibrahim is very much a part of its cultural mix. His aristocratic Javanese mother was born at the ancient Court of Solo, and his father was a diplomat. The designer has made a career helping to redefine what is known as Indonesian style all over the world.

Ibrahim and his partner, John Saunders, base their furniture design and decorating business amid the bustling and overcrowded streets of this busy third-world city. The pair met while Ibrahim was working in England for the New Zealand-born decorator Anouska Hempel, best known for her Asian-inspired London hotel, Blakes. Being in the epicenter of British decorating at the time, the last thing Ibrahim expected was to return home to Indonesia, but on a visit in the '80s he saw more opportunities than he expected in this increasingly prosperous country. New hotels were being built, especially on the nearby island of Bali, with its incoming wave of boutique hotels—and then there were the clients that came with them.

With a sophisticated and studied sensibility, Ibrahim incorporates his influences from abroad in much of his work, but bases it around a deep understanding of traditional Indonesian design. This is evident especially in his small home/office in the Kebayoran Baru district of Jakarta. Constructed in the 1940s, while Indonesia was still a Dutch colony, the bungalow has only four main rooms built around a central courtyard. Ibrahim carefully planned the sight lines to give most rooms a view of this inner space, even raising the height of the doors. Here he also upgraded the traditionally placed bathroom, transforming it into a luxurious indoor/outdoor room. In the center of the courtyard he placed an architectural fragment from a fourteenth-century Javanese temple on a tall stone column, providing a focal point for the whole house.

Like design legend Tony Duquette, Ibrahim adds the unexpected to his walls to give them both formality and texture. On the wall above his bed in the master bedroom hangs a length of his bamboo courtyard fencing, which becomes a graphic background for a selection of framed prints and Ibrahim's collection of small boxes at the head of the bed. Across the room, a Sumba ikat provides a backdrop for an Italian architectural print in a gold frame.

Ibrahim's designs are about display and materials. He uses antique Asian cloths and pottery in Western-style arrangements, and the end result is a cross between museum showcase and the tabletop skills of English decorator David Hicks. In his living room, for example, a collection of fourteenth-century Javanese and Thai bowls on a center table are made even more eye-catching by placing them on plinths cut from ordinary lengths of wood. Despite being in the tropics, Ibrahim's urban base is full of ideas for anyone living in a small bungalow or apartment in a temperate climate.

Carved paneled doors and green glazed Chinese planters flank the entry to the house from the front courtyard. The open fretwork provides ventilation in the tropical climate.

ABOVE: *A fourteenth-century Javanese terra-cotta house temple and lid rest on a couple of tall pedestals. The fabric is an antique Javanese batik.* RIGHT: *The living room walls are green to match the designer's collection of early bronzes. The sofa of his own design sits against the main wall, part of a careful arrangement of shapes and textures, while framed architectural prints help balance the careful proportions of the room.*

Jaya Ibrahim designed the matching cabinets in the living room, which flank a large mirror. The table holds a carefully arranged collection of fourteenth-century bronze bells, bowls, and jugs from Java and Thailand on a round table covered in Tuban fabric from the Nilam Gallery. Cut lengths of wood act as plinths, creating a sculptural composition of varying height. The gold-embroidered nineteenth-century fabric is from Sumatra.

ABOVE: *Antique terra-cotta plant stands sit in a row along the top of a set of cabinets in the office next door to the living room. A couple of chair prototypes in white cardboard on the shelves are from the designer's furniture line.* RIGHT: *Indonesian Art Deco-style chairs surround a dining table covered in white Irish linen, illuminated by a low hanging lamp. The water glasses are capped with lids, Indonesian-style.*

ABOVE: Ibrahim's "tablescapes" have a measured calm. Here, a collection of Indonesian lacquered boxes rests on a table in front of a hanging ikat from Sumba. A Javanese wedding crown adorns the Italian architectural print. RIGHT: The master bedroom walls are red, inspired by the color of Ibrahim's collection of lacquered boxes. Above the bed, he hung a length of his bamboo fencing as a striking backdrop for a selection of framed prints and a collection of small boxes.

ABOVE: Ibrahim designed this daybed and umbrellas in the entry courtyard. The mattress is covered in Sunbrella outdoor fabric.
RIGHT: The master bathroom is given a spalike feel by placing it in the rear open courtyard—only possible in this warm tropical climate. Mirrored screens provide privacy.

BALI HIGH-RISE

John and Cynthia Hardy at the Ansonia, New York

ANY WAY YOU LOOK AT IT, John and Cynthia Hardy are leading extraordinary lives. They have a magnificent, organic open-air house in Bali, built on stilts so that the rice field views and river beyond are still visible. They are also collecting eighteenth-century Javanese wood houses for Bambu Indah, a small hotel the couple has opened nearby. When they realized that their successful jewelry company, John Hardy, headquartered in the middle of nearby rice fields, had grown big enough for a New York base, the couple and their two children were clearly not going to settle for the typical Manhattan postwar three-bedroom apartment.

After much searching, John found a place in the landmark Upper West Side Ansonia building, which is second only to the nearby Dakota in its elaborate Beaux Arts detailing. Its rooms have the high level of craftsmanship and elements of fantasy that the Hardys were accustomed to in faraway Bali. With the help of the late sculptor Aldo Landwehr, John designed almost everything installed in the apartment—and as with his jewelry, he had it made by Balinese craftsmen. Local decorator Anne-Leslie Warren was brought in to take care of the more practical and basic aspects of the project.

A dramatic chandelier hangs in the circular entry area. Lit by candles, it stylistically resembles a Dayak tribesman's version of "gothic" and visually links with a second fixture in the living room next door. Here, a pair of chairs by the Danish designer Hans Wegner adds to an eclectic mix that includes a split bamboo rug and huge finials (or *chofa*) from a Thai temple. Window seats in this curved room provide a view up Broadway that looks little changed since the Ansonia was finished in 1904. The powder room is a real showstopper. With jewel-studded copper walls and fixtures, it feels like a chamber for the gold daleks from the British TV show *Dr. Who*. The open kitchen has a rustic table and chairs, against a backdrop of a large photomural of Mount Batur in Bali taken by John. Here, a Javanese cook makes spectacular Indonesian meals, which adds to the home-away-from-home ambiance of the apartment.

In the master bedroom, a dramatic copper bathtub sits at one end, but the real centerpiece is the large bed made of thick slabs of wood and flanked on either side by Hardy-designed wall lamps. Here, as in the rest of the apartment, the furniture is from Asia—the trunks, chests, and two large wardrobes that stand side by side, sporting headdresses of woven baskets. Any sense that you are in New York completely recedes when you step into the master bathroom. Thick dark wood planks, with the joints lit from behind to resemble daylight, form the walls, floor, and ceiling. The showerhead is concealed in the ceiling so that water cascades down through small holes in the wood, and then appears to gurgle away through the planks. In an instant, you are back in Indonesia—naked in a corner of a wooden Javanese bathroom.

An eye-catching chandelier hangs in the living room. Lit by candles, it stylistically looks like a Dayak tribesman's version of gothic, and links visually with a second fixture next door, which acts as another strong element in the entry.

ABOVE: Like many of the fixtures, John Hardy had these ceiling lights crafted in Bali. A pair of tall Indonesian baskets defines the corridor.
RIGHT: The main rooms lead from a circular entry foyer. Hardy designed the round fur-covered ottoman and rug to echo the shape of the room.

A pair of chairs by the Danish designer Hans Wegner is part of the eclectic mix in the living room, which includes a split bamboo rug and the huge finials (or chofa) from a Thai temple. Window seats in the curved wall provide a view up Broadway that seems little changed since the Ansonia was finished in 1904.

ABOVE: Hardy's company produces housewares as well as jewelry. A silver tray and tea set sit on a sarong—both Hardy designs—in the living room. RIGHT: The handmade wooden dining table is set with Hardy silver, which includes cups and a water jug. The unusual light fixture, like all Hardy products, was also made in Bali.

This small living room provides a private retreat from the rest of the apartment. Natural fiber cushions decorate a low leather sofa. Flanked by a pair of Chinese chairs, a piece of Indonesian tribal art on the opposite wall hangs over a set of Chinese boxes.

ABOVE: *In the master bedroom, Indonesian baskets top a pair of Chinese cabinets that serve as wardrobes. The wood headboard and copper lamps were produced in Bali. A colorful Indonesian textile covers the bed.*
RIGHT: *A dramatic copper bathtub, sent over from Bali, sits under the windows in the master bedroom.*

ABOVE: With copper fixtures and jewel-studded copper walls, the powder room feels like a chamber for the gold daleks from the British TV series Dr. Who. *RIGHT: In the master bathroom, the dark wood planks have their joints lit from behind to resemble daylight seeping in from the walls and ceiling. The showerhead is hidden in the ceiling.*

HIGH STYLE

Eric Hadar's Upper East Side Penthouse in New York, Decorated by Muriel Brandolini

MANHATTAN-BASED DESIGNER Muriel Brandolini's highly personal and stylish decorating is well known all over the world. When New York real estate investor Eric Hadar had unexpectedly picked up a copy of Australian *Vogue*, he knew that she was the right choice to add drama to his extraordinary new penthouse apartment.

Before college, Hadar spent a memorable year traveling around Asia, and Brandolini's Oriental modernism was the perfect look for his new space: offering 360-degree views from the forty-ninth floor of a 1980s skyscraper, it was a fitting aerie for someone involved in Manhattan property, as so many buildings in the city are visible at this height. Brandolini's challenge was to make this "eagle's nest" a comfortable place to live for Hadar and his two children.

The large picture windows in the main living areas are discreetly veiled by elaborate bamboo blinds, which are defined by multiple borders and hung with tassels. They give what could be a rather minimalist apartment a sense of exoticism, which is reinforced by Brandolini's choices of furniture and fabrics. Her color palette echoes the city through the windows, bringing the outside in with a range of blues, beiges, and grays, punctuated by Hadar's art collection, which Brandolini helped him assemble.

Elevator doors lead onto a narrow lobby furnished with a built-in paneled screen and lamps of bronze leaves. Doors open on either side—one to the public spaces, the other to the family areas. In the main living room, a Victorian "conversational," or round sofa, centers the elongated room and sits on a row of circular rugs, joined together with their organic patterns and colors. Brandolini designed Oriental-style divans, which provide three additional seating areas. The contemporary tables and benches in the room contrast with the upholstery, which is often covered with antique textiles. A strong painting by New York abstract artist Peter Halley adds a note of vivid color.

Beyond this space can be glimpsed the screening room, which is furnished again in Brandolini's Oriental modernism. Here, more coffee tables sit on a graphic black-and-white rug. She has painted the walls a pale blue, like the very visible sky seen through the large windows, and the built-in banquettes she designed are upholstered with the same dusty browns as the magnificent cityscape beyond. At night, a screen descends in front of a floor-to-ceiling wooden bookcase that holds a collection of books and family mementos.

Brandolini knows how to knit rooms together by using the sometimes-narrow passageway walls to exhibit detailed ornamental patterns and designs, mainly done by hand. In this apartment, the theme is bamboo, and Brandolini is careful to ground the space with references to nature. In the dining room, the Martin Szekely "ML" dining table sits on a round blue rug from Fedora Design. An organic-shaped chandelier hangs above. The space is divided by a large fish tank. "I love water," explains Hadar, "and I was determined to have an elegant fish tank." Indeed, it is a very surreal experience to look down on the Manhattan skyline through a veil of water with fish swimming past.

RIGHT: A reclining bedroom chaise affords an unparalleled view over Central Park and most of the city. FOLLOWING SPREAD: The main living room includes a Victorian "conversational"— a round sofa. Its shape is echoed by the row of colorful circular rugs, joined together in organic patterns. Muriel Brandolini designed Oriental-style divans that provide three seating areas. A painting by New York abstract artist Peter Halley adds punch to the room.

ABOVE: *A bird sculpture by English designer Francesca Amfitheatrof seems ready to fly over the city.*
RIGHT: *This living room alcove includes slipper chairs designed by Brandolini using Asian textiles. The ornate window blinds add a note of exoticism to the entire apartment.*

ABOVE: *A curved corner of Eric Hadar's daughter's bedroom features shelving to house her extensive collection of dolls from all over the world.* RIGHT: *In the screening room, a pair of Martin Szekely "M.P.V.T." coffee tables rests on a graphic black-and-white rug. Brandolini has painted the walls a pale blue, echoing the view of the sky seen through the large windows. The built-in banquettes she designed are upholstered in the same shade of dusty browns seen in the cityscape beyond.*

ABOVE: *A light fixture by Hervé van der Straeten makes a bold statement in the dining room.*
RIGHT: *Period French chairs surround a Martin Szekely "ML" dining table.*

Brandolini designed the sectional sofa in the family room. A close-up of the family-room sofa shows the Brandolini-designed cushions and a solitary wallpapered wall, which was added to give more interest to the room.

ABOVE: *A Brandolini-designed chair shown against a wall of abacuses, appropriately in Hadar's home/office.* RIGHT: *In the screening room, a screen descends at night in front of this floor-to-ceiling wooden bookcase, which holds books and family mementos.*

ABOVE: *In the master bedroom, the bed has views across the city. Brandolini installed her trademark Asian lamps and pale linens to soften the room. She added natural wood tones to give the space more organic qualities.* RIGHT: *A floor lamp designed by Kim Moltzer makes a dramatic statement in the bedroom.*

MODERN GLAMOUR

Tamara Mellon's London Apartment, Decorated by Martyn Lawrence-Bullard

ATTRACTIVE AND GLAMOROUS, Tamara Mellon is a perfect representative for her shoe company, Jimmy Choo. London-born and American-raised, Mellon started as an accessories editor at British *Vogue* but spotted a niche in the luxury shoe market not quite filled by Manolo Blahnik. Thanks to inherited business acumen from her father, investor Tommy Yeardye, she has since turned Jimmy Choo into a global brand name that represents the last word in chic. As the business exploded into the fashion stratosphere, she needed a larger London apartment, so she moved from Belgravia to a bigger space in fashionable Holland Park, which required sophisticated decorating to reflect her up-to-the-minute lifestyle.

Mellon had been following the career of decorator Martyn Lawrence-Bullard in America, and knew he could give her the drop-dead style she needed. She called him to come help her with the decorating. "I met Tamara Mellon twenty years ago on the then-swinging London party scene," explains Lawrence-Bullard. "She wanted a Hollywood glamour feeling crossed with '70s French style. Very Studio 54 meets Courrèges, with a touch of Holly Golightly." Blessed with a passion for decorating and a boatload of British charm, Lawrence-Bullard is a classic Hollywood decorator, with a client list that reads like an issue of *People* magazine. He gives his clients' houses a sense of theater and drama. "Beauty and diversity are key to good design," he says. These are two principles that inform all of his design work, from textiles to furniture.

Mellon was very inspired by the Hollywood Regency style, which Lawrence-Bullard pumped up with extra pieces from the 1960s and '70s. This eclectic interior combines mirrored furniture from Serge Roche with Venini chandeliers, eighteenth-century Ottoman textiles, and art by Jean-Michel Basquiat. At the same time, Mellon's corporate offices were refurbished by Lawrence-Bullard with a touch of Halston-style 1970s glamour—gold-leaf wallpaper and Paul Evans Cityscape polished metal furniture on wall-to-wall white goatskin rugs.

The large nineteenth-century apartment building's luxurious, hotel-like entry pavilion is a separate structure at the end of a driveway leading to a courtyard garden. The entrance is through a much smaller lobby, with an elevator to the apartment. All of the rooms lead off a large open space acting as a hub for the apartment, which is still a work in progress. At one stage, Lawrence-Bullard reupholstered the furniture in the living room—from pink to a more grown-up brown—and added a cream leather Pierre Cardin Chesterfield sofa, tucked away to provide seating in the corner. Then came more '70s furniture, including elegant coffee tables by Willy Rizzo and Paul Evans. The decorator covered the walls in bold Neisha Crosland and Cole and Son wallpapers, which provide backdrops for photography by Jim Dine and Peter Beard, alongside a strong iconic shot of Brigitte Bardot by Terry O'Neill.

In contrast to the hard-edged '70s furniture in the rest of the apartment, Mellon's bedroom is probably one of the prettiest in London. Lawrence-Bullard captured the essence of her femininity with custom-designed embroidered bed linens made by the Silk Trading Co. in Los Angeles.

A land mine-shaped 1940s Baccarat lighter sits on the living room mantelpiece next to a Venini vase from the 1970s. The artwork is a bronze sculpture by Curtis Jere.

PREVIOUS SPREAD: *In the main living room, a cream lacquer and smoked mirror '60s coffee table by Willy Rizzo centers the room. The surrounding sofas and armchairs were designed by Martyn Lawrence-Bullard. The round sculpture by Curtis Jere repeats the shape of his wall piece hanging above.*
ABOVE AND RIGHT: *A Fornasetti vase and a 1970s Stuben sculpture sitting on a glass coffee table give sparkle to the living room. The chairs are by Paul Evans, from his Cityscape collection. The Warhol is an original screen print of Grace Kelly.*

LEFT: *A Peter Beard photograph hangs above a Jansen desk along the wall of the living room. The chair is by Jacques Adnet.* ABOVE: *In the dining room, a Paco Rabanne table is surrounded by dining chairs by Adnet. A colorful 1960s chandelier in Murano glass by Seguso hangs above it.*

The master bed is covered with beautiful custom linens from the Silk Trading Co. The nineteenth-century textile hanging on the wall behind was found in Istanbul. A pair of vintage lamps by David Hicks flanks the bed. A Mongolian lamb fur rug from the Rug Company adds a touch of luxury underfoot.

ABOVE AND LEFT: *In Tamara Mellon's daughter's room, a large vintage* suzani *found in Istanbul's grand bazaar continues the pink theme. The rug was designed by Lawrence-Bullard for the Rug Company.*

INTERNATIONAL STYLE

Robert Couturier's Home/Office in SoHo, New York

FRENCH DESIGNER ROBERT COUTURIER has always done "big." One of his first projects was the huge, 60,000-square-foot Cuixmala estate for Sir Jimmy Goldsmith in Mexico—and that was just the main house. By contrast, the elegantly dressed decorator's own apartment in New York's fashionable SoHo district is a pied-à-terre, which has morphed into his business office. There is a gradual transition past the entrance and through the double doors, from home to office, where distant assistants can be seen hunched over computers, surrounded by piles of fabric swatches.

Couturier's personal work area is located in the middle of the apartment, which during the day functions as a glamorous head-of-the-company space, with Jacques Adnet furniture and Léger tapestries. The bedroom, bathroom, and dressing room are hidden from view behind discrete curved walls, hand-painted by artist Paulin Pâris.

A pair of overscale white statues of Roman muses, bought from the Andy Warhol estate, dramatically flanks the elevator doors, which open directly onto the apartment. No space is wasted: the entry can double as a dining room, with its elegant Savin and Adnet table, or provide space for occasional client meetings. Suede upholstered Jansen dining chairs outlined in red paint add to the sophistication of the setting. When the doors to the office are closed, this room has a different rhythm and ceases to be just a passageway.

In the living room, apart from the large photograph of Couturier by Gerald Incandela and a pair of chrome armchairs from the 1970s, you could easily be transported to 1940s Paris—much of the furniture is by Adnet. This famous French furniture designer is known for his luxurious take on modernism. His pieces are used today by designers to give a touch of glamour to modern interiors.

Couturier's desk is set into an alcove with a view of the main living space, where a flat-screen television doubles as a client presentation tool. What sets this space apart from the typical home office is its appointments—no printers set on packing cases here. As the French designers of the 1940s revolutionized office furniture, all the important design houses decorated the interiors of commercial buildings, as well as residential spaces—the elegance of their desks, cabinets, and chairs remains unmatched.

The staff departs at the end of the day, leaving behind Kugel, the office cat, who loves all the activity. Weekends are really quiet here for the rather overfed black cat, as Couturier departs for his large country house in Connecticut, on sixteen acres, complete with an octagonal library, which overlooks a peaceful lake. Here the designer has a chance to step back from the office in the city and think about the future—which includes projects in New York, a large Lutyens house in England, an apartment in Paris's 7th arrondissement, and a house in the Caribbean.

A tapestry by Fernand Léger hangs above a pair of elegant French chairs from the 1970s in the central sitting room. The walls were painted by Paulin Pâris.

A Gerald Incandela portrait of Couturier hangs above the living room sofa by Adnet. It is flanked by a pair of eighteenth-century Chinese bookcases.

ABOVE: *Perfect for a pied-à-terre, behind a curved wall is a small but luxurious bed, backed by a Jean-Michel Frank-style screen.*
RIGHT: *Couturier's desk, by Adnet, is tucked into an alcove with a view of the main living room. The TV can double as a client presentation screen.*

ABOVE: *A ceramic sculpture by Jean René Gauguin, son of the famous painter.*
RIGHT: *The bathroom features glass tile from Bisazza and a useful zebra-skin ottoman.*

DAKOTA MODERN

Leslie and Sean Goodrich's New York Apartment,
Decorated by Muriel Brandolini

IT IS NOT A STRETCH TO SAY that the most legendary apartment building overlooking Central Park in New York is the Dakota. Built in 1884 by the architectural firm of Henry Janeway Hardenbergh, the Dakota was constructed with its own private electrical power plant and central heating. It set the standard for luxury New York living at the time, and its vast inner courtyard has the feel of a small European town plaza.

Several years ago Leslie and Sean Goodrich were lucky enough to find a place here, and they asked decorator Muriel Brandolini to rework their new duplex apartment. Both being in the financial business, they had no time to travel with her to Europe on shopping trips, so they needed to trust her judgment. This was not a problem for Brandolini—she is happy to work this way, confident in her own singular taste and sensibility.

Although located on the ground floor and smaller than the usual apartment in this building, the space nonetheless has the fine nineteenth-century proportions that this landmark building is famous for. Better still, it has a stunning view of the park at almost eye-level and the constant fascinating parade of people passing by.

Brandolini reversed the conventional order of rooms in the apartment. At first sight, past the entryway and the downstairs staircase (upholstered with colorful words, like a giant art installation) sits a "Marie Antoinette"–style bed—a four-poster silk confection draped in a Cowtan & Tout fabric, in what should be the living room. It is illuminated inside by a hanging bird sculpture, made by English designer Francesca Amfitheatrof. This placement immediately gives a sense of poetry to the apartment.

Large open doors lead to a muted gray-green living room, which reflects the greens of Central Park across the road, like water in a pond. A Brandolini-designed coffee table, inspired by Samuel Marx, rests on a blue-green Fedora Design carpet; it is surrounded by Brandolini sofas, her signature square slipper chair, and a wicker chair by Marc Newson. The conversation stopper, however, is around the corner in an upstairs dining room—a wall filled with the couple's amazing collection of pottery by French ceramicist Roger Capron. Capron worked side by side with Pablo Picasso in Vallauris, France, during the 1950s, and his work shows Picasso's influence. Brandolini decided to showcase the pieces on shelving of her own design that was constructed by City Joinery. They sit like an art installation, overlooking a Brandolini table, which is curved to allow more seating in this relatively smaller room.

The downstairs has been transformed into a combined family room, with space to accommodate the dog and a new baby. Cleverly worked into the stairwell is a built-in wine rack. Beaded sentences punctuate the gray fabric used to upholster the walls. A comfortable seating area is screened from the kitchen, with storage room under each built-in sofa; a dining table sits en route to several bedrooms that open past an upholstered archway. This floor was a design challenge, as it is basically a basement with one window, but Brandolini has added a collection of sophisticated visual ideas, which transform this awkward space into an attractive part of the apartment.

Brandolini designed the curved table in the dining room. The abstract, boxlike shelving holds a collection of pots by French ceramicist Roger Capron—an ideal way to display the Goodrichs' extensive collection.

The apartment's fine proportions are
evident in the living room. Brandolini
designed the sofas, coffee table, and slipper
chair. The Marc Newson wicker chair is
from Galerie Kreo in Paris.

RIGHT: *A Martin Parr photograph overlooks a kitchen table by Dutch designer Piet Hein Eek. The table is surrounded by Italian chairs from the 1950s. A detail shows the walls covered in felt, punctuated by hand-beaded words from Lou Reed's song "Perfect Day."*

A dramatic silk-draped
four-poster in the
French style anchors
this bedroom, for
which Brandolini chose
a Cowtan & Tout
fabric. It is lit by a
bird sculpture poetically
positioned above the
bed, made by English
designer Francesca
Amfitheatrof.

*ABOVE: A Pierre Paulin lamp makes a sculptural statement.
RIGHT: Reflecting the colors of the bedroom, the owners' collection
of Rosenthal glass from the 1960s is lined up on the mantel.*

ABOVE: In the entrance stairwell, beaded words are again used as a unique wall decoration. This time, the words were from songs by the Rolling Stones.
RIGHT: Artwork by Jenny Holzer is an appropriate choice for the word-studded wall downstairs in the media room. The stainless-steel mesh divider separates this room from the kitchen. Brandolini designed the sofas to have storage under the seats.

MODERNIST STYLE

David Cruz and Richard Hochberg's Schiff House, Los Angeles

IN THEIR HOLLYWOOD HILLS HOME, David Cruz, co–owner of the quintessential L.A. furniture store Blackman Cruz, and music writer/theater director Richard Hochberg have sensitively adapted a modern classic to suit the twenty-first century. Designed by architect Paul László in 1939 for the Schiff family, the house sits on a slope. The bedrooms lead unexpectedly off the main entrance at street level with dramatic views over Hollywood's nearby downtown district. Below, the living area is open and spacious, with a broad, south-facing balcony that extends the full width of the house, an area that is used year-round, especially for open-air dining.

The only area that they have really changed is the kitchen, which was opened up with the help of designer Jane Hallworth, who also worked with Cruz to create the muted colors in the rest of the rooms. This used to be the maid's domain, and Hochberg always worried about creeping claustrophobia whenever he had to cook. Opened up, the kitchen now has a city view, but is hidden from the living room by a corner wall.

As a composer, Hochberg's shiny new black grand piano was essential for his work, but it looked wrong in this 1939 house. So Cruz bought him a vintage upright piano by Danish furniture designers Hornung and Møller, and he obligingly had its interior almost entirely rebuilt. Today it sits in the "California" room, a paneled bar room designed to be closed off with a glass pocket door in case anyone needed to smoke.

But it is the furnishings that add the final touch to this elegant house. Cruz draws from his store's collection of famously eclectic furniture, and the house is filled with his current enthusiasms, often discovered on buying trips around the world. In the living room, two rare French leather chairs from the 1960s or '70s (Cruz isn't exactly sure), upholstered with brick-shaped leather pieces, sit in front of the fireplace. They flank a spacious László-style coffee table that is home for many of the design books the couple collects. It doubles as a storage center that is as spacious as a bookcase. This room looks through to the dining area, which is centered by a striking Blackman Cruz dining table (part of their collection of new furniture) that is surrounded by Italian Carlo di Carli chairs upholstered in black patent leather. An early-twentieth-century Japanese screen hangs on the wall behind a wooden French sofa decorated with embroidered antique textile pillows.

Upstairs in the master bedroom, the bed has a quilted leather coverlet, and the bed skirt and pillows are made from antique textiles. The black fur throw and under-blanket tie in with the room's black wood paneling. Unlike many modernists, the couple is not afraid of furniture showing its age, and they have no qualms about correctly leaving original upholstery and finishes. In the corner, Cruz keeps his favorite piece of furniture: an exotic early-twentieth-century Carlo Bugatti chair, found unexpectedly in Mexico City. The bedroom seems bigger than it actually is, because it opens directly onto a broad balcony overlooking the city.

But don't imagine anything here is for sale—Cruz carefully guards his collection. Only once during the Blackman Cruz's recent move to a bigger store in Hollywood did Hochberg notice an attrition. However, it didn't take long for the house to fill up again. As the gentle city breeze wafts through the large steel-framed open windows, their elegant and carefully worn furniture sits comfortably and harmoniously.

In the living room, a French sculpted bronze head from the 1930s rests on a console table from the same period.

The dining area, with windows overlooking Hollywood, is anchored by a sleek "OP" table from the Blackman Cruz workshops. A 1940s oak sofa from France provides seating along the wall, and a graphic early-twentieth-century Japanese screen hangs above it.

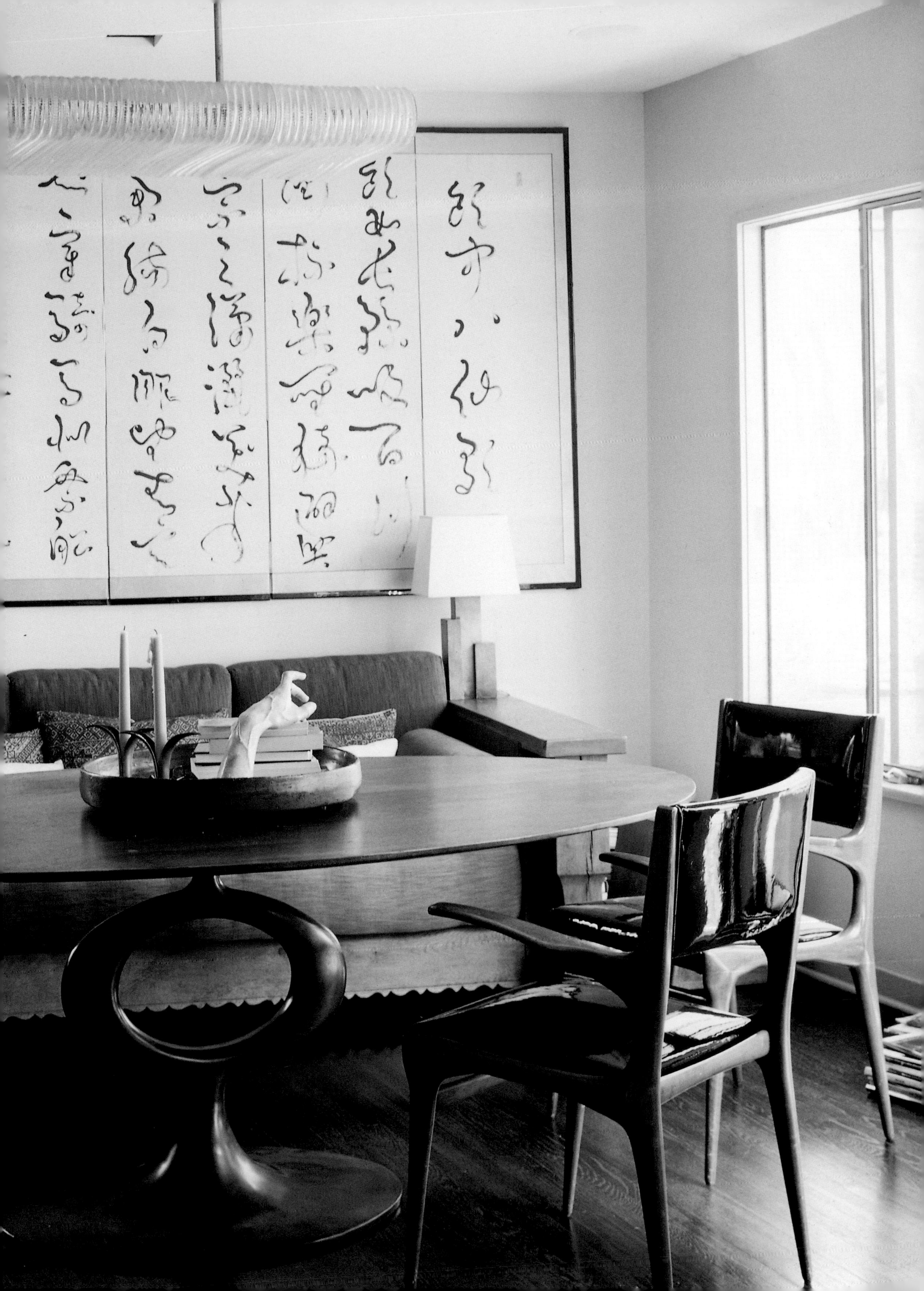

ABOVE: *In the main living room, two unique French leather chairs upholstered with brick-shaped leather pieces sit in front of the fireplace. A Paul László-style coffee table doubles as a storage space as spacious as a bookcase. This room looks through to the dining room.* LEFT: *In the TV room, a collection of nudes hang on the wall. An Italian glass "Aella" lamp from the 1960s sits on a side table beside a de Sede leather sofa.*

ABOVE: *This city house is entered at street level, and stairs descend to the main living areas.* RIGHT: *At the bottom of the stairs we can see the original grooved banister. A vintage architectural model of a staircase sits on an adjustable table.*

ABOVE: *A vintage upright piano in the "California" bar room, by Danish designers Hornung and Møller, was a gift to Hochberg from Cruz.*
LEFT: *In the bedroom, the eye is drawn to an early-twentieth-century Carlo Bugatti chair, found in Mexico City.*

ABOVE: *A hanging eighteenth-century gilded mirror is reflected in the mirrored master bedroom wall, adding glamour. A luxurious dark fur throw covers the bed.*
RIGHT: *The wall-mounted bedside table was found at a French flea market.*

PREVIOUS SPREAD: One living
room wall is covered with an
eclectic collection of paintings
with a flat-screen TV that
unexpectedly becomes part of
the assemblage. Photographs
by William Wegman, Robert
Mapplethorpe, and Horst hang
next to assorted flea-market finds.
RIGHT: The dining room does
double duty as the library. The
large white table is surrounded by
Adler's Chinese Chippendale
chairs in a bright green, which
matches the window blinds. A
vintage 1960s chandelier acts like
a piece of jewelry for the room.

ABOVE: *Vintage green-and-white wallpaper brightens the master bedroom walls, and the touches of yellow continue a color theme found throughout the apartment. White furniture and molding keep the room feeling fresh.*
RIGHT: *Daughter Anna's bed is incredibly pretty, with pink gingham bed curtains and a matching lampshade trimmed with white bobbles. Washable vintage wallpaper featuring cats and mice in bright candy colors cover the walls.*

FRENCH CHIC

Sean Mathis and Florence de Dampierre's New York Pied-à-Terre

DECORATOR AND AUTHOR Florence de Dampierre has been promoting French chic for most of her glamorous life in New York. The stylish de Dampierre first arrived from London in the mid-1980s and opened Florence de Dampierre Antiques, a store with bright red walls, specializing in painted furniture from the eighteenth and nineteenth centuries. At the time decorators and collectors were tiring of stuffy, over-gilded period pieces, and the color and humor of painted furniture was a refreshing alternative. Sadly, the store is no more, as de Dampierre, married and raising young children, decided to work from her country home and pursue a career as a decorator.

Although based in Litchfield, Connecticut, the couple also keep a pied-à-terre in New York, where de Dampierre has thrown the decorating rule book out the window and decided to just have fun. Color pervades all of her projects. Her Connecticut front door is easily spotted from the street by its vivid lime green, one of her trademark colors. In New York, her pied-à-terre is a vision of pale green and lilac. In her recent book *French Chic*, de Dampierre advises that "nothing creates greater height and depth than a ceiling painted in pale aqua...do not be afraid of color—it is one of the most effective and economical ways of decorating a space."

The apartment, in an Upper East Side mid-century modern building, has plenty of light. De Dampierre chose it because it has windows on two sides, with views across the city. The front door opens onto a combined living/dining room. A second bedroom functions as an office that Florence and Sean use when they are in the city. A pair of sofas in the living room folds out for the children's occasional visits.

A great believer in decorating with both high- and low-priced elements, de Dampierre happily uses Crate & Barrel chairs at a table set with French Sèvres plates and lime green plastic glasses to add an element of surprise and whimsy. "French chic is not only about spending money," explains de Dampierre. "It is about using your knowledge to invest wisely in quality, and to create a setting that fits your personality and lifestyle." The pastel colors of her apartment are reminiscent of French Ladurée macaroons, which contrast with the gritty New York streets downstairs. Inspired by her interest in painted walls and furniture, de Dampierre's next book will be on decorative wall surfaces.

In the main living space of the small apartment, a Karl Springer dining table rests on a Pottery Barn rug, surrounded by colorful Karim Rashid "Oh" chairs.

CLOCKWISE FROM TOP LEFT: *The bedroom view includes the spire of the church of St. Elizabeth, a neo-Gothic structure built in 1893. A bright and fun table setting assembled by Florence de Dampierre. Added to the colorful walls is a botanical painting by Elizabeth Thompson. As a nod to her book on chairs, de Dampierre hung this small watercolor by Garouste and Bonetti in the study.* RIGHT: *De Dampierre designed these cut-out felt leaves, which she uses here as a tieback.*

HOLLYWOOD REGENCY

Mary McDonald's Los Angeles Guesthouse

DECORATOR MARY McDONALD loved the "bijou" qualities of her Hollywood Regency-style house in West Hollywood so much, she couldn't bring herself to sell when it was time to look for a new home. Instead, she was resourceful enough to be able to transform it into a guesthouse, even though it is miles away from her new place. McDonald uses the guesthouse for entertaining friends, but it is also a perfect laboratory for this constantly evolving designer, and it photographs like a dream.

The pretty gray-and-white facade of the 1940s bungalow opens almost directly onto the street. Inspired by houses in the Caribbean, McDonald installed shutters, added palm trees to the small garden, and placed a gazebo at the top of a minuscule, sloping patch of lawn. Inside, the entry space is anchored by a broad, book-filled table. McDonald painted the ground-level floors a glossy white, defining each area with a dark brown border. The entry opens onto a black-and-white living room decorated with bold strokes; its monochromatic hues are enlivened by an unexpected pink curtain trim framing the windows.

The daring gray-black and emerald green dining room has an added rich gold wallpapered ceiling, which gives shimmer to the space. This color scheme works because the white floor and pale upholstery on the chairs provide a fresh contrast to a color combination that would otherwise be overpowering. McDonald often shops with a certain color in mind, which provides a collection of objects that add punch wherever she arranges them.

Through to the kitchen, a small breakfast nook shows the sure hand of a confident decorator.

Metallic zigzag Osborne & Little wallpaper hung with graphic numbered plates would be enough for most people, but McDonald adds faux-snakeskin upholstered chairs, a sleek white Saarinen-style table, and a modern pendant light for extra oomph.

Upstairs, a master bedroom suite is decorated in crisp navy blue and white, with a hand-painted sisal rug. Next door, McDonald created a chinoiserie-inspired guest room. Here, an inventive headboard is paired with crisp white Chinese-style figures, reminiscent of 1940s design magazines. "These silhouettes are just projected on the wall and then painted in," explains McDonald.

While most people would settle for a rudimentary basement, furnished perhaps with a little-used Ping-Pong table, here McDonald took advantage of the doors opening onto the garden and transformed this floor into a guest suite with its own entrance. The living room follows a simple plan: bright rainbow stripes of color painted on the back wall are toned down by the white furniture and neutral sea grass carpet. She links this decorating scheme with the graphic wall design by using similarly colored fabrics on a variety of pillows and cushions. McDonald tented the guest bedroom on this floor, which is an ideal way to treat a small room, insulating it from noise and making it cozy at the same time. A basic palette of beige and gray is freshened up by the use of pale blue in the blinds fabric, cushions, and mats for the chinoiserie prints that hang on the wall. A side table against the wall has been transformed by a graphic coat of painted stripes. From top to bottom, McDonald has filled this city house with great ideas, based on a sophisticated eye for shape and color.

RIGHT: Elegant stairs inside the entryway lead up to two of the bedrooms.
FOLLOWING SPREAD: The floors on the first floor are white, with the living area defined by a dark brown border. The black-and-white living room is decorated with bold strokes. Monochromatic hues are enlivened by splashes of the unexpected pink curtain trim framing the wall.

The living room looks onto the entry area, where a wool-skirted table, useful for displaying design books, anchors the space. A nineteenth-century Chinese cabinet with gilded inlay adds shine to the room.

A bold palette of black, red, and gold adds punch to the entry area. The photograph is by Miguel Flores-Vianna.

Allure   Diana Vreeland   BULFINCH

138

ABOVE: *The outfit worn by the model in this 1960s Mark Shaw photograph inspired this dining room's green motif.* RIGHT: *The gold Cowtan & Tout wallpaper on the ceiling adds shine to the dining room, as does the crystal chandelier, which reflects light from the garden. The dark gray-black and emerald green is an inspiring combination for the room.*

*In the master bedroom,
Mary McDonald kept
to the dark blue-gray,
refreshed with the pink
palette of the living
room, but added a
hand-stenciled sisal rug
to give the room a lift.*

ABOVE: The bathroom continues the color scheme of the adjacent master bedroom, but in much paler tones. The seersucker-upholstered settee adds a sense of comfort to the room.
RIGHT: An unexpected bright pink ceiling inside the draped bed provides a refreshing jolt of color.

ABOVE: *This guest bedroom is a chinoiserie-inspired fantasy. The graphic figures were made by using a projector to create shadows on the wall and then filling in the outlines. McDonald designed a "quilted pagoda" headboard.* RIGHT: *Osborne & Little "Volte-Face" zigzag wallpaper adds drama to the small breakfast nook. Black faux-snakeskin-covered chairs and graphic numbered plates give a skillful balance to the room. The Saarinen-style white table and modern hanging lamp provide a calm counterpoint.*

Downstairs, the basement has been transformed into a glamorous and comfortable media room. McDonald had the walls striped and then added fresh touches of white and green to the furnishings. A photograph by Mark Shaw, with a broad white matting, was chosen to give a note of feminine chic.

HOLLYWOOD AT HOME

Peter Dunham and Peter Kopelson's West Hollywood Bungalow

DESIGNER PETER DUNHAM, owner of Hollywood at Home, a chic fabric and vintage furniture store, has made the most of his small West Hollywood bungalow, built in 1928. Despite its size, Dunham and his partner, dermatologist Peter Kopelson, loved the charming Spanish-style house at first sight—Kopelson grew up in a similar home in Beverly Hills, while Dunham has childhood memories of his parents' summerhouse in Cadaqués, Spain.

Although French was his first language (Dunham grew up in Paris), he quickly learned English at school in the UK. Here, he met his great friend Ashley Hicks, son of the legendary decorator David Hicks. "His father was the first decorator I ever met. I thought, how could I be a decorator like him? The shadow was long from the people I had met," explains Dunham. "I moved to L.A. from New York to be with Peter and thought it would be a hobby . . . It evolved into a real career when our first house was published, as I realized that I had become a decorator."

Dunham also sells his own fabrics. "I started by doing fabrics for my clients as I couldn't find what I wanted. I have always loved antique textiles, and liked that look." Dunham adds, "I have always loved the geometry in Islamic things and the rhythms of fabrics." Today his collection can be found at both Hollywood at Home and John Rosselli in New York.

With the bungalow, Dunham's aim was to make a comfortable urban home for himself, Kopelson, and their four dogs. Conveniently, the large garage, built in 1939, had previously been turned into another living space that the couple reworked into a guest room below and an office above. In the main house, the front door opens directly into a spacious living room, which has a direct line of sight to a marble bust on a plinth in the garden at the far end of the property. To the right of the living room is the dining room, which doubles as a library, with a table piled high with books. The impressively large ceiling lights here came with the house and were originally rescued from a theater downtown. The room's "Fig Leaf" blind fabric by Dunham was inspired by a visit to Salvador Dalí's house, near his parents' home in Cadaqués. The dining chairs were bought from a sale of Hollywood props featured in the 1953 classic film *How to Marry a Millionaire,* and are now part of Dunham's furniture line. "Quintessential Hollywood at home, that's what Los Angeles is about. The old Hollywood modernism, which is so romantic, is what my store tries to convey," he says, which is reflected in the decoration of his own house.

A second living room opens onto the back garden. Dunham enlarged the space, taking out a small foyer and replacing it with a fireplace and a wall of bookcases. A corridor leads to the added master bedroom, which overlooks the pool. Parts of the previous spaces then became walk-in wardrobes. The imposing bed was part of the original furnishings, and Dunham has covered it with a large *suzani*. The blue curtains are made of another of his fabrics, this time a nod to his mentor Hicks.

It would be hard to improve this well-thought-out house. However, as we all know, there is always one more project waiting: "I plan to redo the kitchen and make it larger—combining it with the dining room and opening it onto the front lawn so that we can use that part of the garden more," says Dunham. He hopes this will be the final refinement of their indoor and outdoor spaces, as there is not much left to work with. But who knows where such creativity will strike next?

Plates by Greek artist Konstantin Kakanias hang on the entryway wall. The fabric on the nine-foot sofa is "Antigua Stripe" from Chelsea Editions.

ABOVE: *An African tribal shield adds to the room's eclectic decor.*
RIGHT: *An impressive white pot rests on a column base by the door to the back garden.*

An overscale nineteenth-century photograph of Rome is a striking element in the main sitting room, where Peter Dunham has used many of his own fabrics. He chose grass wallpaper from Hinson & Company to disguise the drywall look of this recent addition to the house. The rug was woven from a sketch by Ernest Boiceau, the designer of his parents' Paris apartment.

ABOVE: *A treasured photograph of English aristocrat Stephen Tennant hangs on the bookshelves in the combined library/dining room.* RIGHT: *Dunham found the dining room chairs at a movie-set sale. The impressive ceiling lights—previously from a downtown theater—were here when they moved in. The room's "Fig Leaf" blind fabric by Dunham was inspired by Dalí's house near his parents' home in Cadaqués.*

Dunham added beadboard to the walls of the guesthouse that had been converted from a garage years ago. These living room wicker chairs from Hollyhock, in West Hollywood, are upholstered with "Fig Leaf" fabric by Dunham.

map for a chicer future.
(besides your nearest...)

BEVERLY HILLS
SANTA MONICA BLVD   cuz the tech meets the glam
DOHENY   ROBERTSON
        MELROSE   AVENUE   SAN VICENTE

Hollywood at home
636 N. Almont drive, Los Angeles, CA 90069

The large master bed
came with the house.
Dunham chose a bold
suzani as a bedcover.
The curtain and blind
fabric is from his own
line, and adds a note of
extra color to the room.

162

EMPIRE LINES

Liv Ballard's Parisian Pied-à-Terre

WHENEVER LOS ANGELES-BASED jewelry designer Liv Ballard thought of Paris, she fondly remembered her life there as a student over twenty years ago. Marriage and motherhood had interrupted her travel plans, but when her children grew older she was finally able to return to France with her family for Christmas. Before you could say *bienvenue*, Ballard found a charming but tiny one-bedroom apartment in a seventeenth-century building facing a courtyard, across the Seine from the Louvre. It didn't need much work—mostly painting and furnishing. Ballard brought me in to give her a hand, as I had worked on the family's Beverly Hills house. (Although she certainly didn't need any help with her French.)

We flew over to tackle an unknown contractor, who in typically Parisian fashion treated us to a nice long lunch. After a glass or two of wine, it dawned on us that this was going to be much easier than we thought. Because the apartment was so small, we replaced the cupboards on either side of the living room fireplace with large French doors mirroring the windows opposite; curtained and lit from behind, they give the illusion of another courtyard beyond.

Since the apartment is on rue Bonaparte, we decided to incorporate a Napoleonic theme. Ballard found four nineteenth-century inlaid ebony chairs by George Bullock in San Francisco, which now stand in the living room. Bullock, an Englishman, made furniture for Napoleon when he lived in exile, and these four chairs, with seats covered in striped pink silk, fit the theme nicely. The only piece of furniture bought in Paris was the eighteenth-century ebony inlaid armoire in the living room, which we lined in pink silk to match the chairs. It serves as a useful media cabinet.

Although furniture was brought in from both the United States and the UK, the color choices had to be made in Paris, as the quality of light was too subtle to make any real decisions in Los Angeles. With cool sunlight flooding the apartment, warm pinks and reds soon became obvious choices for the main rooms. The tiny kitchen, more like an afterthought in restaurant-filled Paris, is shoehorned into a sunporch that has windows lined with blue stained glass. Added to match the nineteenth-century glass, blue crystals dangle from the chandelier and crystal wall sconces that light the entrance hall. We found a red crystal Montgolfier light fixture in London, which now hangs in the main bedroom over an exotic Portuguese bed, shipped over from West Hollywood. The curtains were made from a Chelsea Textiles hand-embroidered and bordered linen.

The contractor unearthed a honey-colored nineteenth-century wooden spiral staircase to access the mezzanine, a tiny space that now serves as a bedroom for the Ballard boys. We squeezed in a metal trundle bed from the same period and incorporated a Napoleonic theme here, too, making free use of the emperor's bee motif. Then we hung the boys' bedroom with fabric so that the whole resembles a large draped bed.

With everything in place, the family arrived for summer, suitcases filled with bed covers and comfortable American-style pillows—only to find there was no hot water, thanks to an unlucky upstairs neighbor whose pipes had burst. But, upon reflection, they quickly realized that this, too, was part of the Parisian experience.

An eighteenth-century French armoire anchors the living room and provides a place to house the flat-screen TV. It is lined in pink to match the chairs upholstered in linen from Diamond Foam and Fabric.

*ABOVE: On the chimneypiece sits a silver lamp discovered on a shopping trip to London.
RIGHT: The fireplace and gilded mirror are original to the apartment. A Moroccan
chair covered in pink striped fabric sits next to the sofa with a hand-sewn red trim. The
floor is covered with an apple-rush mat from England.*

ABOVE: *A set of pink-and-white china and a nearby lamp were found in London. The nineteenth-century table is made of ebony.* RIGHT: *The nineteenth-century inlaid ebony dining chairs by George Bullock and matching ebony table are drawn together when needed for casual meals.*

ABOVE: *Ballard's two sons share a tiny mezzanine, which we draped like a large bed, and installed a metal trundle bed with a lower pullout for the youngest.*
RIGHT: *The master bedroom has an exotic Portuguese bed, covered in Chelsea Textiles fabric. Above hangs an antique Montgolfier chandelier found in London.*

ABOVE: *A detail of the bedroom curtain fabric—"Gooseberry Border" from Chelsea Textiles.* RIGHT: *"June Street" chairs from Hollyhock in Los Angeles are the perfect choice for a small room. They are comfortable as well as compact.*

ABOVE: *The chandelier and wall sconces in the entry area were augmented with extra blue glass to match the kitchen windows.*
RIGHT: *Light shines through the nineteenth-century blue stained glass of the tiny kitchen, which was created out of a small sun porch.*

A SOPHISTICATED PALETTE

Fashion Designer Zang Toi's Town House Apartment, New York

WHEN FASHION DESIGNER Zang Toi first spotted the elaborate fin-de-siècle facade of his New York town house on the Upper East Side, he was thrilled. The elegant gray stone building looked as if it had been spirited from Paris's 7th arrondissement completely intact. Today, at first glance the interior of his apartment looks like an elaborate confection of ornate nineteenth-century–style furniture and crystal chandeliers, but upon closer inspection it is clear the space has been stripped down to an almost military precision.

The color scheme is black, white, and silver—which requires great organizational skill to maintain. (Patterned paper towels—certainly not!) All the utility rooms have been reduced to closet-size: Toi's impeccably tailored clothes hang in immaculate formation in one, and in another, a small, neat black desk with a couple of computer screens takes up all the available room. A mirrored space leading off the entry contains a chic black massage table, and the kitchen, done in white marble, is hidden behind a set of folding doors in the living room. This leaves the generous and beautiful proportions of Toi's two-room apartment unspoiled by unnecessary clutter. As a result, the space appears larger, and the French-inspired turn-of-the-century moldings and panelling give grace and dignity to the rooms.

Many layers of glossy white wall paint add a contemporary feel, especially when paired with the heavily lacquered black parquet floors. In the living room, this minimal color scheme serves as a background to Toi's Louis XVI-style furniture, which he hasn't hesitated to paint white and silver, and upholstered in Loro Piana cashmere. Anchored by a large silver-fox–fur rug that is centered in the room, two seating areas sit back to back, creating a hip formality. Above the fireplace, Toi has hung a combination of two mirrors, which add extra shimmer to his color palette. Reinforcing his take on French culture, a pair of monochromatic portraits of Marie Antoinette, commissioned by Toi from American artist Natasha Zupan, flank the chimneypiece. Toi loves Paris. "Sometimes I fly there overnight and visit for twenty-four hours. I stay in my favorite hotel, the classic Hotel Ritz on the Place Vendôme, dine at Le Grand Véfour, and come right back home again!" explains the designer with a flash of his famous charm.

Family photographs in black and white (naturally) are elegantly displayed in an ornate white cabinet opposite the fireplace. In elaborate nineteenth-century silver frames, they are carefully and formally placed, which suits the style of the room.

Filling the center of the bedroom is a pedigreed nineteenth-century bed that is flanked by windows, which, like those throughout the apartment, are in the French style, with folded-back shutters and silver espagnolette bolts. Apart from a pair of discrete black bedside tables, and matching Toi-designed black side chairs, the rest of the room is empty. In keeping with the designer's sense of minimalism, there are no paintings hanging on the walls.

These rooms are a long way from Toi's birthplace in tropical Kelantan, in Malaysia. However, there is something of a colonial formality about them. Toi was knighted by the Sultan of Malaysia, and his apartment is very much the home of an aristocratic fashion designer of the twenty-first century. "I'm so happy with it," he says. "After a long hard day at work, I love to come home."

One of a pair of large paintings of Marie Antoinette by American artist Natasha Zupan that hang in the living room refers to Zang Toi's enduring love of France, which inspired the decoration of this apartment.

ABOVE: The elaborate silver candlestick ties into the black, white, and silver color scheme of the apartment. RIGHT: Even though Toi decorated the living room with period furniture, it still feels modern, thanks to its glossy paint surfaces and simple color scheme.

ABOVE: This large antique cabinet at the back of the living room came with the apartment. Toi had it painted a glossy white, and in keeping with the color scheme of the apartment, placed black-and-white family pictures with silver frames inside.
RIGHT: Here you can see the fashion designer's sophisticated use of fabric. Toi covered the furniture with Loro Piana cashmere, including the ottoman, which doubles as a coffee table.
FOLLOWING SPREAD, LEFT: The small master bathroom is paneled in white marble to create an atmosphere of luxury. RIGHT: The bedroom has very little superfluous furnishings. The nineteenth-century bed has been lacquered a glossy black.

WELL-TRAVELED CHIC

Carolina Irving's Upper East Side Apartment, New York

WHEN THE IRVING FAMILY left their Beaux Arts converted ballroom apartment for this chic but more child-friendly Upper East Side space, it wasn't much of a sacrifice as here the main living area is fifty feet long. Nonetheless, it still took work for Carolina and her husband, Ian, to refine this colorful and personal space that today she shares with her two daughters, Olympia and Ariadne.

First, they brought in architect Daniel Romualdez to rework the original three front rooms into an open space, with separate areas defined by half-height bookcases. Gothic molding was added—perhaps acknowledging the beautiful Roman Catholic Church of Saint Jean Baptiste next door—contributing to the apartment's exoticism.

Carolina grew up in Paris. She has early memories of her stylish Venezuelan parents' stunningly beautiful Jansen-designed apartment there. Having worked as a stylist and editor for various magazines, including *House & Garden*, Irving eventually produced a textile line of her own, as she loves fabric. This passion is clear throughout the apartment. Textile finds from Egypt, India, and Morocco are intermixed with her own designs, as well as the occasional bits and pieces from John Robshaw, and friends Peter Dunham and Ashley Hicks.

The entrance to the apartment is filled with many treasures. A late-seventeenth-century English tapestry portrait taking up the end wall gives the space an added dimension, making the windowless room seem larger. There are plenty of convenient chairs to set a shopping bag on, and a pair of facing tables display many of Irving's exotic finds, like opaline lamps from Paris's Clignancourt flea market. From here, a passageway leads to the master bath and the bedrooms. In her own bedroom, Irving was inspired by the great French decorator Madeleine Castaing and used her wallpaper with vertical stripes to add height to the room. Piles of books and fabrics give the space a lived-in feel, while the tall shimmering aqua-blue silk curtains create drama.

In the book-filled main living room, Irving has added lots of comfortable, family-friendly armchairs and sofas slipcovered in her favorite fabrics. A pair of big stone Celtic heads, bought from famed collector Alistair McAlpine, adds a rustic touch. His regular column on the last page of each *World of Interiors* for many years is a must read. The most useful piece in the room is a large Robert Kime octagonal ottoman, which centers a seating group of chairs and a sofa. The rug, a blue-and-white striped dhurrie from Jaipur, defines the space in a strong graphic way, and the color links each corner of the room together. Irving studied art history and archaeology at the École du Louvre in Paris, and it shows in her reading choices here, with subjects that range from Pablo Picasso to exotic and remote Asia. It would be incredibly easy to spend weeks curled up with them in one of her cozy sofas. She is a true cosmopolitan, as comfortable in Europe as she is in Latin America. However, it is the lure of the Middle East that she finds the strongest—a passion she shares with her great friend, shoe designer Christian Louboutin. They sail the Nile together in his houseboat and "walk everywhere."

RIGHT: A seventeenth-century portrait of Margaret Arundel, Lady Weston, attributed to Robert Peake the Younger, hangs in a corner of the opened-up living room behind a 1760s German beaded table. The chair is Louis XV.

PREVIOUS SPREAD: A blue-and-white dhurrie rug from India links the living room with the dining room/library beyond. A large ottoman from Robert Kime doubles as a coffee table. A beaded Italian chandelier hangs above the dining table. ABOVE: The large Mexican portrait hung over an Indian textile provides scale to a comfortable corner of the living room. RIGHT: One of the bookcase dividers serves as a base for a large faience urn. This over-scale element stops the room from seeming cluttered.

ABOVE: *A featherwork shield of Venezuela, where Carolina Irving spent part of her childhood, hangs above an oversize Louis XVI daybed, with cushions by Ashley Hicks. The silk ikat used as a covering on the right is from Uzbekistan.*
RIGHT: *A detail of six mezzotints from Thomas Frye's Gallery of Beauties, based on women of the time, which hang on the living room wall.*

ABOVE: *In the entry hall, a nineteenth-century urn decorated with shells and flowers rests in front of framed scenes of eighteenth-century Dresden. The blue lamps are from Paris's Clignancourt flea market.*
RIGHT: *At the end of the entry hall, an antique English tapestry gives the space an extra sense of depth. Cartoons for Georgian silver hang on the walls, which are upholstered with green baize.*

ABOVE: *The gothic armchair in the master bedroom is upholstered in a*
Le Manach textile. Piles of Irving's own fabrics can be seen on the sofa. The bright
blue curtain picks up the color in the striped Madeleine Castaing wallpaper.
RIGHT: *Silhouettes of Irving's two daughters by Elliott Puckette hang over the bed.*

STAGE PRESENCE

Peter Hinwood's London House

IT WOULD BE NEARLY IMPOSSIBLE to create an apartment like antiques dealer Peter Hinwood's without years of traveling and collecting. This is not an instant, showroom-like interior hurriedly pulled together in a week or two. Regular trips to Tangier, where he has gone for years, have been the source of many of Hinwood's finds, and their air of exoticism permeates the entire living space.

His first venture in the London decorating world was to work for legendary antiques dealer Christopher Gibbs. Eventually, they became partners in the business, and the apartment you see here is a result of all those years of work. It was previously the drawing room of a large eighteenth-century house once inhabited by the Speaker of the House of Commons, and it came with elegant proportions and plenty of wall space.

Here, Hinwood has hung an eclectic collection, including African shop signs, nineteenth-century Indian botanical paintings, a late-fifteenth-century Venetian portrait or two, and even a seventeenth-century carved and painted moosehead trophy that belonged to Elizabeth of Bohemia. However, Hinwood kept the wall colors bright to banish any hint of museum-like stuffiness.

Up an elegant curving staircase, a small entryway painted Moroccan blue opens onto the apartment, which leads on the left to the drawing room and on the right to the bedroom. A "hidden" door conceals the bathroom, which is aptly indicated by a Qajar portrait of a Persian beauty taking her bath hanging overhead. The drawing room has an impressive eighteen-foot ceiling, painted a pale sky blue so that it almost appears to merge with the sky outside. This room is the result of years of obsessive shopping. A richness of detail is unified by the Moroccan blue-green walls and a spectacular eighteenth-century eight-fold screen on the walls from Macao showing a profusion of dogs, birds, and cocoa trees. Small Moroccan stools around the room link the space together, and large mirrors provide scale to counterbalance the many small discoveries displayed in cabinets and on countertops.

The green-painted master bedroom is anchored by a centrally placed brass bed, draped at one end with a red, white, and blue Ewe cloth from Ghana. Hanging above the bed are pieces of folk art from Africa, including a barbershop sign. Admits Hinwood, "To tell the truth, I'm much more likely to be turned on by the atmosphere of something from an African shantytown than a grand country estate." On a nineteenth-century simulated bamboo chest of drawers a large Lin-Can canned fruit container has been reused as a lamp base. Hinwood keeps a balance by scattering far less precious finds around the apartment, and most of his upholstery and curtain fabrics come from utilitarian Moroccan parasol suppliers.

In the kitchen, an eighteenth-century English painting of a cat and lobster hangs appropriately above the stove. It is surrounded by a Moroccan child's pigeon poster, various watercolors of fruits and flowers, and odd nineteenth-century photographs. Hinwood resourcefully employed black-and-white butcher's shop tiles on the walls as a gesture toward practicality.

Back in 1975, Hinwood played one of the leads in the *Rocky Horror Picture Show*, which changed the lives of everyone who appeared in it. However, over the years he has created a different persona in this very personal and densely layered London apartment.

Against the living room window, Peter Hinwood placed a seventeenth-century green pottery jar from Spain. Displayed on the desk is an album of geometrical drawings and watercolors of tile patterns throughout the Arab world.

ABOVE: *In the living room, on an eighteenth-century marble-topped English side table by William Bradshaw is displayed a collection of Turkish tiles and an antique jardiniere made up of Iznik fragments. Above it hangs a 1913 painting by Sir John Lavery.*
RIGHT: *Hanging on the door of the bathroom is a nineteenth-century Qajar portrait of a Persian beauty taking her bath. A sculpted section from a massive antique Roman urn rests on a green-painted, eighteenth-century marble-topped Irish table. Above it hangs an Irish white-painted architectural mirror.*

PREVIOUS SPREAD: *The multiple collections in the living room are anchored by a late-seventeenth-century Persian carpet. The room is a glorious mixture of antique tiles, Chinese jars, pictures relating to Tangier, Moroccan low tables, and an elk's head above the drawing room door that once belonged to Elizabeth of Bohemia. The early Victorian armchair is covered in bold striped cottons found at a Moroccan parasol maker's workshop.*
RIGHT: *In this comfortable corner of the living room, the cat pillows echo the English Regency tabby cat portrait on the wall. A large oval English Regency mirror overlooks the sofa. Above it stretches a dramatic eight-paneled eighteenth-century Chinese screen from Macao.*

ABOVE: *In this corner of the living room, Hinwood displays a fifteenth-century brass Mamluk* hammam *basin on an English marble-topped table from circa 1730. Above it hangs a fifteenth-century Italian "fish" portrait.* RIGHT: *Hinwood's extensive collection even invades the kitchen. The room is dominated by a group of watercolors, including an eighteenth-century painting of a cat and lobster. Graphic black-and-white butcher's shop tiles line the bottom half of the walls.*

ABOVE: *In the bedroom, striped green curtains made from heavy cotton bought from parasol suppliers hang in the windows. On the wall is William Hodges's magical period painting of a tropical garden. On top of the nineteenth-century simulated bamboo bedside table from Woburn Abbey, England, sit an eighteenth-century Chinese jar and a Moroccan striped pot with a lid.*
RIGHT: *The brass bed is by James Shoolbred. Next to it, a large Lin-Can canned fruit tin is used as a lamp base. A large early Asafo flag, from Ghana, hangs below an African barbershop sign. Draped over the end of the bed is a red, white, and blue Ewe cloth from Ghana.*

PART II

City Decorating

STORING AND DISPLAYING BOOKS

IF YOU ARE READING THIS, you most likely collect design books. Today, there are beautiful and well-produced books available on every conceivable topic—from garden follies in Europe to breathtaking interiors and individual decorators' work, both past and present. And with today's high publishing quality, they are harder to resist than ever before. Every year aficionados buy at least four or five to browse through for pleasure as well as for decorating ideas and to make fun new discoveries.

Therein lies the problem. Where to put all these books? Today's small city apartments make it hard to find a place to store them, and many books are too large for conventional bookshelves. There are many practical solutions—if you have an infrequently used dining room, utilize it as a library; the dining table can even do double duty as a place to spread out books. Floor-to-ceiling bookcases on all four walls should be enough to hold most people's collections. A guest room is another ideal place to keep books. Why not ensure that your friends are never short of a good book to read? Bookcases can be squeezed into all sorts of unexpected places, underneath dormer windows or concealed in an armoire. A thoughtfully arranged pile of books can also look good on the floor at the foot of the bed, whether underneath or stacked carefully on top of a useful upholstered bench. In the living room, piles of enticing and colorful books can lure you into a comfortable sofa for the rest of the day. They can be stacked on ottomans and footstools, or arranged in towers on the floor. Place a bowl or a small statue on top of a stack, to give a sense of purpose. Big baskets are another great book and magazine storage idea, and a matching set on either side of a desk even looks organized.

If going without shelves is too untidy, you can always install bookcases and call any room the library and be done with it. Why not buy an antique bookcase? Often they can be purchased for the same price as carpenter-built shelves. They look better, and you can take the bookcase with you if you move. A large *secretaire*, whether antique or modern, can also be filled with books and kept in almost any room.

Bookcases and shelves can be squeezed into all sorts of unexpected places. Sometimes a landing or entryway can become a mini-library. Here, make sure that the built-in shelving reaches the ceiling and is topped with the same molding as the walls, to create a seamless effect. Plan for high and deep shelving at floor level to take in larger books, while paperbacks and novels can fill smaller spaces at the top. Keep in mind that large coffee-table books do best stored flat, while walls of books often look better with their dust jackets removed.

There are endless creative ways of incorporating books into a decorative scheme, and into limited city living areas. After all, remember the old adage—"Books furnish a room." Still have a space problem? After you have donated the ones you don't want to the library, the sentimental favorites that you will never read again should be boxed, labeled, and stored. It is as simple as that.

PREVIOUS SPREAD: Decorator Russell Bush loves design books—they fill his Park Avenue home/office in New York. One of a pair of treasured nineteenth-century chairs from the great French decorator Madeleine Castaing sits near the table. RIGHT: This double-height wall inventively serves as a giant bookcase in collector Michael Boyd's house in Los Angeles.

ABOVE: *Decorator Kelly Wearstler uses this central table to define the space between the living and dining areas in her Los Angeles house. It also becomes a handy place for books and magazines.*
RIGHT: *Separating the main living/dining room is a double-sided bookcase that decorator Alex Papachristidis found in one of the many antiques shops in Hudson, New York. It is the perfect way for a book-lover to divide a long, well-lit space.*

ABOVE: *A corner of Russell Bush's apartment, showing how stacks of books can make great side tables.* CLOCKWISE FROM TOP LEFT: *A decorative object placed on a pile of books cleverly turns them into a plinth. Bookcases should reach the ceiling. Here in the author's house they are defined by crown molding and painted the same color as the walls. In his Spanish Colonial West Hollywood apartment, storeowner Dan Mary has added old books as decorative objects to create this bookcase tableau. Peter Dunham uses his books as a backdrop for one of his favorite photographs of the eccentric Englishman Stephen Tennant.*

In the town of Litchfield, Joseph Montebello and Ron Leal converted each wall of their dining room into bookcases, creating an elegant and sophisticated room that works in both a city apartment or country house.

LEFT: *Decorator Tom Beeton made the most of existing niches in his West Hollywood bungalow to creatively arrange some of his books.*

CLOCKWISE FROM TOP LEFT: *Bookcases can be built in stair landings. Here, French decorator Jean-Louis Deniot took advantage of some extra space in his small apartment to house his book collection. Bookcases can be used for display as well as storage. Collector Michael Boyd shows some of his museum-quality library of twentieth-century design books. An entry table is a convenient place to keep current books. Here, they can be easily picked up and read. The interior design is by Peter Dunham. A music system speaker is cleverly disguised as a row of books.*

ABOVE: *An eighteenth-century ottoman at the home of the author is used
as temporary book storage, doubling as a way to display china.*
CLOCKWISE FROM TOP LEFT: *Though usually used to display china, an English
secretary cabinet was also intended to house books. A bedroom can also function
as a library. Here, designer Andrew Virtue has added to the books a decorative
collection of small boxes. This sitting room and library was carefully designed by
Martyn Lawrence-Bullard so that the tops of the bookcases are level with that of the
windows. These small details give a room a professional touch. Kelly Wearstler was
inspired by Tony Duquette when she designed this malachite green library in her
Los Angeles home. Here, she left plenty of room for her growing collection of books.*

CITY KITCHENS

THE KITCHEN, A HIGHLY FUNCTIONAL part of a city house is often the most versatile room of all, even if—as is the case for many busy urban dwellers—it is just a space for unwrapping take-out.

In a big city, especially like New York, there may be very little space for food preparation, the pressure of city life often means less time to prepare meals, and restaurants are often conveniently close by. However, it is a mistake to neglect this room. Take time to design your kitchen. Done well, there are few things that can improve an apartment more than a well-organized and attractive cooking space. There are only a few design rules to bear in mind, so don't be intimidated. The distance between the refrigerator, stove, and sink is called the "triangle," which refers to the typical food preparation area. Keep this area compact, as you want to be able to move as quickly as possible between these three locations—especially with hot food. Work out how many people will use the kitchen, how many meals will be prepared here, and how much space is needed. If two people will be cooking together, and you have plenty of space, ideally two sinks should be part of the plan, twin food-prep areas should be designated, and two garbage disposal sites should be nearby.

If you plan on entertaining, or have a big family, I would suggest space for two dishwashers. And a large freezer placed in an adjoining room, such as a pantry, would certainly be welcome. When you plan your kitchen, allow for as much counter space as possible. Hang as many cabinets as you can—the more storage, the less clutter on useful workspaces. Some cooks like open shelving, which allows them to grab what they need quickly, while others want closed doors for a tidier look. However, if you have little more than a passage to work with, remember that some of the best cooks in the world have tiny kitchens. Alternatively, many people prefer to open up the kitchen so that it becomes part of the living space. This is a big step that should be carefully considered, especially as future owners may have a different way of life, where the clutter of dishes and pots are best left hidden. Bear in mind also that too much lighting can be obtrusive and unnecessary. Supermarket-style brightness can take away the happy intimacy of preparing food together as a family. Under-counter strip lighting can illuminate most food preparation areas, and a few hanging fixtures are useful to add drama to the space—a chandelier or two over a kitchen island adds more than just light.

There is a huge industry dedicated to kitchen fittings and appliances, and the best way to begin is to be as minimal as possible. The most successful kitchens are integrated into the rest of the home and match the style: if you have used plenty of wood in the living room, then do the same in the kitchen. Or if the apartment is in an old prewar building, then keep to the same look with white "brick" tiles on the backsplash and a marble countertop. Resist the temptation to go overboard with colored tiles and fancy hardware—a fussy kitchen in someone else's taste will be a stumbling block to a successful resale in the years to come. You can always personalize your kitchen with art, wall colors, and fabrics that can easily be changed. There is a big trend currently for industrial-looking appliances, often in stainless steel. Since this look is widely available, prices are relatively low. Today, you can get stoves, ovens, dishwashers, and refrigerators from several different low-cost manufacturers—you would be surprised at how many attractive and economical choices there are.

If you have the luxury to be able to fit a breakfast table in the kitchen, do so: it can be one of the nicest places to spend the morning. Sitting around drinking coffee, gossiping, and reading the paper can be a rare pleasure in a fast-paced urban world.

Gently distressed surfaces add character to this well-designed kitchen.
A table serves as a central kitchen island.

*ABOVE: This elegant modern kitchen is by Steve Hermann, who is notable for his skilled
use of materials. Notice how the marble backsplash extends right up to the ceiling.
RIGHT: Collector Michael Boyd renovated his kitchen to recapture the 1960s mood of the
house's Brazilian architect, Oscar Niemeyer.*

ABOVE: *A collection of antique glass jars used in stores to hold candy, combined with other useful flasks and sugar shakers, form an attractive display in decorator Martyn Lawrence-Bullard's kitchen.* CLOCKWISE FROM TOP LEFT: *An antique dresser makes a convenient and attractive piece of kitchen furniture in the Paris kitchen of 1stdibs founder Michael Bruno. This clever storage system uses the space on the back of the cabinet doors. Architect Troy Adams created a sophisticated modern food-prep area. The soft green of the walls provides a background for the white china displayed in an open cupboard.*

This urban kitchen has been opened up to the ceiling by designer Tom Callaway, and was decorated by Windsor Smith to be a big, comfortable family room.

CLOCKWISE FROM TOP LEFT: Designer Tim Clarke opened this kitchen up to the family room while keeping a sense of separation for the busy cook. Richard Rouilard recognized the charm of his period kitchen in the Hollywood Hills and simply added a fresh coat of paint. Designers Beverly Archer and Robert Bernard designed this Pasadena kitchen with open storage—The attractive, neat rows of food supplies show how this can be a decorative feature. A useful and artistic display of cooking pots. Designer Kathy Guild shows how decorative an old stove looks in a crisp, well-designed kitchen. Clean, scrubbed pots in the Qualey home form a composition on a handy open-storage rack. Skillful design makes this wood cabinetry both practical and beautiful. Martyn Lawrence-Bullard kept the charming original kitchen in his 1920s Spanish Colonial home in the Hollywood Hills, adding marble cutting boards that flank the period stove.

CLOCKWISE FROM TOP LEFT: *Peter Dunham designed this room with a workspace that doubles as a dining table. John and Debbie Stall's brief was to create a kitchen for keen bakers, where raw materials are readily available. This kitchen island, designed by designer Steven Brady, makes a very convenient place to store china as well as provides a useful surface area. A decorative and functional pot rack.*
RIGHT: *When David Cruz renovated his kitchen, he confined the appliances and cupboards to one massed corner of the room to save space.*

ABOVE: *This cool, modern kitchen by KAA Design Group includes a large window to bring the outdoors inside, which grounds the space.* RIGHT: *Filmmaker Jan Sharp's Los Angeles kitchen has a South Asian feel. She recycled antique Indian cupboards to craft the cabinets. The tiled floor was imported from Morocco. "Kitchen" Ming plates from Indonesia are displayed on the wall.*

PREVIOUS SPREAD, TOP LEFT: David Cruz's sympathetic renovation of his 1939 kitchen by Paul László included plenty of natural wood detailing. BOTTOM, LEFT: This white kitchen by designer Jeff Andrews was given a lift with an exotic ceiling light. TOP, RIGHT: Counter stools add a graphic accent to this kitchen by Tim Clarke. BOTTOM, RIGHT: For her own house, Kelly Wearstler took the idea of a stainless-steel kitchen and made it glamorous. ABOVE: Muriel Brandolini encouraged a client to personalize his kitchen table. A hanging rack of pots makes it easier to cook while an extra counter separates the space. RIGHT: This warm red kitchen is the heart of the Wagman apartment, decorated by Jonathan Adler. The wall is covered with marble, giving the backsplash a clean look.

ENTERTAINING IN THE CITY

NO ONE EVER REALLY KNEW how the famous entertainer Elsa Maxwell did it, but she planned the best parties, with a creative mix of people and music. She staged them as theater, which was a lot easier in the 1930s, '40s and '50s when people actually drank and could be persuaded to do crazy things like word games and costume parties. A short, overweight middle-aged woman with no money and only a moderate ability to play the piano, Maxwell nevertheless managed to become one of the most successful party-givers of her generation. Following in her footsteps, many of us can do the same, especially if we can entertain in an impromptu and informal way, and like her, can make the best of what we have. Elsa Maxwell always provided some sort of entertainment, even if only by playing the piano (or today's version, an iPod), which kept the party going.

We all have the right spot for a party, no matter how small an apartment may be. A memorable evening can start with just a pretty table surrounded by practical and comfortable chairs, and set in front of a window, or wherever the most interesting view can be found. A round table encourages conversation, where extra guests can always find a place. Today it is easy to buy tablecloths, napkins, and dishes in bright designs in very economical stores like Target and Pier 1. You can use antique porcelain with colorful, inexpensive glasses as a way to mix things up.

Lay the table with a creative mix the day before if you can. Start with a centerpiece. Most flower vases are too high—people don't like being hidden by elaborate and tall arrangements. A cluster of little arrangements or small vases is often more successful than a single large one. Remember that you don't always need to use flowers—bright colorful fruits or vegetables can look just as interesting and are often more original. Piles of yellow lemons or green grapes that match the tablecloth are cheerful and welcoming; in the fall, combine pumpkins and squash together with piles of colored leaves. A centerpiece is also the chance to make the most of small collections of objects like shells and objets that you have picked up over the years. Almost anything that is amusing or charming will do—even toys.

Another time-saver is place cards, as they solve the awkward question as to where to sit at the table. This gives you more time for other chores. They can be written in colored ink on nearly anything small—nuts, shells, or leaves provide a chic organic touch. Place cards let everyone know where he or she is to sit while you cart the food from the kitchen. Set the meal out on a nearby buffet table. It is much easier for guests to get up and help themselves than to be served.

The secret of stress-free party planning is preparation. Reintroduce the dining room, if you have one, as a "dedicated" space for entertaining, and stock the pantry, refrigerator, and cocktail bar with basics to always have on hand for guests. If you are busy all week, complete one task a night and by the weekend you will find yourself organized and ready to go. At the end of a successful evening, you will have provided your friends with a priceless moment or two to laugh, enjoy themselves, and escape the stresses of the outside world. Hopefully you will have a great time, too.

A cool modern dining table in Los Angeles—the bright orange of the chairs is the statement here. The room was designed by Guy Cnop.

Hutton Wilkinson decorated this table at Dawnridge in the style of his mentor Tony Duquette. There are no limits to the centerpiece here—Wilkinson believes it encourages conversation among neighbors when they can't see across the table.

LEFT: *The authors' Asian-inspired table, laid with inexpensive decorations from Pier 1, joining a collection of eighteenth-century "Kitchen" Ming from Indonesia.*
CLOCKWISE FROM TOP LEFT: *A table set for breakfast makes an inviting corner of the kitchen. Martyn Lawrence-Bullard designed this beautiful table, drawing on his collection of antique glass and accessories.* BOTTOM RIGHT: *A casually chic decorated table by Peter Dunham, based on a tablecloth in one of his own fabric designs. Flowers that match the tablecloth give a sense of balance to a set table.*

Designer Kate Stamps decorated her dining table in Pasadena with eighteenth-century glassware and china, adding a simple vase of flowers from the garden.

ABOVE: *The authors' table in a central courtyard. Hand-painted Italian Cama Deruta china is paired with glasses from Pier 1.* RIGHT: *Californian garden designer Nancy Power added a fireplace to her outdoor dining area. Here she uses a blue tablecloth with colorful green plates and purple napkins.*

CLOCKWISE FROM TOP LEFT: *The authors' table set with various flea-market finds, including nineteenth-century American glassware. Inexpensive glasses from Pier 1 are combined with inherited nineteenth-century blue-and-white china on the authors' dining table in Hollywood. Colorful glass purchased at flea markets brightens a table set with antique creamware. Hermès china mingles with small pineapples—a symbol of hospitality—on a small table in Martyn Lawrence-Bullard's Hollywood Hills kitchen. Decorator Andrew Virtue shows how a rooftop or garden tent can be furnished like a formal dining room. A candlestick by Picasso lends glamour to Lawrence-Bullard's outdoor breakfast table. Comfortable wicker chairs and a witty chandelier give this dining alcove personality. Candlesticks from Lawrence-Bullard act as a centerpiece on a table for two by a sunny window.*

ABOVE: *Storeowner Dan Marty furnished his dining room with comfortable chairs from his own line, available at the Pacific Design Center store, and upholstered them with antique red linen.*
RIGHT: *An informal dining table created outside on a small terrace in Lawrence-Bullard's Hollywood home. The statue is an eighteenth-century gilded bronze Quan Yin altar ornament, and the ruby glass decanters with gold-leaf decoration are Russian, circa 1820.*

DESIGNER DIRECTORY

The following architects, interior designers, designers, and antiques dealers have homes or design projects featured in this book, and several have their own furnishing lines and shops.

Jonathan Adler
Jonathan Adler Interior Design
212-645-2802
www.jonathanadler.com
For interior design projects, contact info@jonathanadler.com.

Thomas M. Beeton Associates
917-288-2087
www.beetonassociates.com

Muriel Brandolini
167 East 80th Street
New York, New York 10075
212-645-5940
www.murielbrandolini.com

Russell Bush
4 Park Avenue
New York, New York 10016
212-686-9152

Thomas Callaway Associates
2920 Nebraska Avenue
Santa Monica, California 90404
310-828-1030
www.thomascallaway.com

Robert Couturier
69 Mercer Street
New York, New York 10012
212-463-7177
robert@robertcouturier.com
www.robertcouturier.com

David Cruz
Blackman Cruz
836 North Highland Avenue
Los Angeles, California 90038
323-466-8600
www.blackmancruz.com

Florence de Dampierre
P.O. Box 1576
Litchfield, Connecticut 06759
FdeDampierre@aol.com
www.frenchchic.org

Jean-Louis Deniot
Cabinet Jean-Louis Deniot
30 rue de Verneuil
Paris, France 75007
33-1-45-44-04-65
www.deniot.fr

Diamond Foam and Fabric
611 South La Brea Avenue
Los Angeles, California 90036
323-931-8148
www.diamondfoamandfabric.com

Peter Dunham
909 North Orlando Avenue
Los Angeles, California 90069
323-848-9900
www.peterdunham.com
and
Hollywood at Home
636 North Almont Drive
Los Angeles, California 90069
310-273-6200
www.hollywoodathome.com

Tony Duquette, Inc.
Hutton Wilkinson, President
P.O. Box 69858
West Hollywood, California 90069
310-271-4688
www.tonyduquette.com

John Hardy
Green School at the Kul-Kul
Campus
Jl. Raya, Sibang Kaja
Banjar Saren, Abiansemal
Badung 80352
Denpasar, Bali
Indonesia
62-812-388-3888
John@johnbalil.com

Jaya Ibrahim
www.jayainternational.com

Carolina Irving
Carolina Irving Textiles
80 Church Street
Englewood, New Jersey 07631
646-688-3365
info@carolinairvingtextiles.com
www.carolinairvingtextiles.com

Martyn Lawrence-Bullard
Martyn Lawrence-Bullard Design
8101 Melrose Avenue
Los Angeles, California 90046
323-655-5080
info@martynlawrencebullard.com
www.martynlawrencebullard.com

Dan Marty
Dan Marty Design
Pacific Design Center
8687 Melrose Avenue, Suite B380
West Hollywood,
California 90069
310-652-6928
info@danmartydesign.com
www.danmartydesign.com

Mary McDonald
Mary McDonald, Inc.
9165 Phyllis Street
Los Angeles, California 90069
310-246-1307

Alex Papachristidis
Alex Papachristidis Interiors
300 East 57th Street, Suite 1C
New York, New York 10022
212-588-1777
www.alexpapachristidis.com

Paulin Pâris LLC
Art & Design
4501 West Jefferson, Unit A
Los Angeles, California 90016
323-737-1822
www.paulin-paris.com

Kate Stamps
318 Fairview Avenue
South Pasadena, California 91030
626-441-5600
www.stampsandstamps.com

Tim Street-Porter Photography
323-549-0122
www.timstreet-porter.com

Zang Toi
30 West 57th Street
New York, New York 10019
212-757-1200
www.houseoftoi.com

Andrew Virtue
VIRTUE Interior Design
5318 East 2nd Street, Suite 698
Long Beach, California 90803
562-856-1789
www.virtueinteriors.com

LEFT: *A detail of a stool in Muriel Brandolini's apartment for Eric Hadar.*
RIGHT: *The front door of Zang Toi's nineteenth-century apartment building on New York's Upper East Side.*

First published in the United States of America in 2010
by Rizzoli International Publications, Inc.
300 Park Avenue South
New York, New York 10010
www.rizzoliusa.com

2010 2011 2012 2013 / 10 9 8 7 6 5 4 3 2 1

Printed in China

ISBN 13: 978-0-8478-3430-3

Library of Congress Control Number: 2009940392

Project Editor: Sandra Gilbert
Art Direction: Doug Turshen with David Huang